DRIVEN

THE DANNY EDWARDS STORY

Champion Professional Golfer

Race Car Driver

Entrepreneur Extraordinaire

✦ ✦ ✦ ✦ ✦

Developer/Founder of Royal Grip Inc.

President of the Tour Players Association (TPA) that achieved change to the Tour's approach to governance

with Bob Denney

FOREWORD BY JOHNNY MILLER

CLASSICS OF GOLF
The world's best reading golf books.

CLASSICS OF GOLF

Classics of Golf
50 Gedney Street
Nyack, New York 10960
845-765-6050
classicsofgolf.com

First Classics of Golf printing, 2022

Classics of Golf is a registered trademark.

ISBN 978-0-940889-69-9

Library of Congress Cataloging-in-Publication
Data on File

For contact or ordering information write:
info@classicsofgolf.com

Cover: Getty Images

Manufactured in Canada

To my parents, Frank and Donna Mae Edwards,

for providing a peaceful, supportive, challenging and spiritual home

environment that inspired me to pursue excellence.

And to my wife, Mery, for sharing a passion

for the game of golf, patience, and loving support.

CONTENTS

✦ ✦ ✦ ✦ ✦

FOREWORD

✦ ✦ ✦ ✦ ✦

If I had not chosen golf, I would have liked to have been a builder or developer. I owned more than 50 assorted properties, my favorite being western ranches. I love being outdoors, developing and beautifying things.

Danny Edwards shares a similar passion for evoking change in everything that he has been associated with, from transforming himself without a coach into a PGA Tour professional, to handling a race car at breakneck speed, to founding a business that would revolutionize a segment of the golf industry to standing tall as a coach with answers to the Chipping Equation.

When I turned professional at age 22 in 1969, Danny was a high school senior in Edmond, Oklahoma, and won the state golf championship. That milestone came three years after he was introduced to golf by watching youngsters hit balls on a football field.

It's only natural that a guy like Danny, who fast-tracked learning how to swing a golf club, would apply the same energy toward what was really burning inside him: the quest for speed.

Danny was just as at home behind the wheel of a hot car as he was strolling the fairway. While his golfing peers were honing their games on the practice tee, Danny was contemplating the next race and how he would navigate the track. Racing wasn't just a pastime for him. It was in his DNA, and he went on to win his share of races and one significant national event.

As our respective PGA Tour careers intersected, Danny stood out for how precise he was in approaching golf. He wasn't hard to pick out on the course—he was the one who dressed sharply and looked like he was born for the role of a golf professional.

You must have tons of talent, combined with unbridled enthusiasm and a lot of hard work to get to compete at the Tour level. That's what Danny had, and it's remarkable when you consider where he started and what he achieved in his career.

Danny's life journey is a fascinating read. You'll find he has a great memory for documenting some unforgettable stories that will both surprise and entertain.

I didn't know until Danny reminded me that he was midway through his final round on June 17, 1973, at Oakmont during the U.S. Open when he heard whispers around the course that I had shot 63. There wasn't social media or ESPN at the time, of course.

Danny was always brainstorming new ways to do things. That resulted in a five-year career in competitive golf for at the same time he was breaking new ground in business.

Danny brought the precision and focus he applied on the course to his founding of Royal Grip Inc. in 1988. By finding the missing pieces to the puzzle of making a better product, he shook things up in a highly-competitive industry. That is really living the American dream.

On October 13, 1985, Danny and I were paired in the final round of the Walt Disney Oldsmobile Classic. He was on a tear. He had a back nine 6-under par 30 and finished with a 66. What made that round interesting is that he putted while looking at the hole. He said it was his attempt to improve his putting.

I was so energized watching him making putts from everywhere that I had to give it a try back home.

Incidentally, that same day, Danny and I heard whispers of another exceptional performance. Lanny Wadkins won in Disney World with a course record-tying 63.

Danny's memoir of a unique life is a study of what a nonstop, focused, workmanlike effort can yield. He chronicles the ups and downs he has experienced and how they have shaped his driven life.

I believe that anyone who wants to be successful will find a little bit of Danny in their life. He remains an inspiration for all those willing to take a chance and realize that golfers—yes, golfers—can extend their vision and excel beyond the boundaries of a course.

—**JOHNNY MILLER**

October 2021

Pacific Grove, California

PROLOGUE

✦ ✦ ✦ ✦ ✦

When I tuned into the 1973 Open Championship at Troon Golf Club and watched Tom Weiskopf finish a wire-to-wire victory, I had no idea who the bushy-haired young man sitting in a chair by the 18th green was. Moments later, a Royal and Ancient official presented that young man with a silver medal as Low Amateur.

Two milestones merged at twilight that day at Troon. Weiskopf was presented the Claret Jug as the Champion Golfer of the Year, enjoying his lone major in a career that overlapped with fellow Ohio State University alum Jack Nicklaus. And Danny Edwards completed his improbable maiden trip to the United Kingdom and golf's oldest major.

His success in the Open Championship was part of Danny's magical amateur career. He won the 1972 North and South Amateur at Pinehurst No. 2 and the Southeastern Amateur in Columbus, Georgia, and was runner-up in the Porter Cup, Eastern Amateur, Dixie Amateur, Sunnehanna Amateur—many of the cream ports of call of this country's amateur circuit.

Danny qualified for the 1972 U.S. Open at Pebble Beach Golf Links and nearly made the cut. He celebrated his 21st birthday the Wednesday of the Open.

As the years passed, I discovered more about Danny, who spent 14 full seasons on the Tour while also becoming a skilled race car driver. Danny has a strong Christian faith, and my guess is that it is advantageous to have an angel in your pocket navigating a sweeping right-hand turn at more than 100 miles per hour or negotiating a major championship venue under the scrutiny of tens of thousands of spectators. To come close to mastering both athletic disciplines is a marvel in itself, even if not a result of divine intervention.

Danny's combination of athletic ability, hand-eye coordination and split-second reflexes also enabled him to do something in 1982 that no other professional golfer has accomplished—win a PGA Tour event and follow that triumph a couple months later by capturing a national automobile race.

There has to be something special about a golf professional whose horizons for achievement extend far beyond the course. Consider Danny's birthplace, for example. He was born on June 14, 1951, in Ketchikan, the southeasternmost major settlement in our largest state. Alaska comprises a fifth of the entire United States. It takes seven days to cruise its shores, and more than a year to see it in its entirety.

But Danny and his mother spent just three months in Alaska before a tuberculosis scare among the Native Americans in the region sent them packing shortly after his birth. They found a safe haven in Kansas City, the first of two stops for the family before they settled for good in Edmond, Oklahoma, in 1960.

In 2017, FOXSports.com ranked Danny as Alaska's greatest golfer. Although Alaska's golf season peaks from June through September in a state featuring more than thirty-five courses, and although he lived there for such a short time as an infant, Danny's career in the game and his contributions to the industry justify such recognition.

Growing up in a town that had no golf courses and in a family that had no golfers, Danny became a golfer.

It happened while he was a starting point guard on the Edmond High School basketball team and earned all-state honors his senior year. That same Edmond Bulldog mentality that he exhibited in being the best on the court—staying well past closing time in the gym to practice his jump shot—he carried outdoors to golf.

While team sports have their allure, golf was a giant magnet for Danny.

He didn't have a father to coax him or pass on a few fundamentals. There were no golf professionals in Edmond.

His "coaches" were television stars—including golf's Big Three of the 1960s: Arnold Palmer, Jack Nicklaus and Gary Player. Danny spent weekends in front of the TV watching the best in golf execute on a course he could only imagine. Generations before technology dominated instruction, Danny was focused on his own black-and-white virtual practice tee.

In 1969, three years of hard work paid off as Danny won the Oklahoma State High School Golf Championship. He earned a golf scholarship to Oklahoma State University, which boasted one of the premier collegiate golf programs in the nation. In this book, he will fill you in on his relationship with the wily and legendary Cowboys coach, Labron Harris Sr.

Danny's work ethic was at odds with an unofficial policy that freshmen should remain "gradual climbers" in the ranks of a renowned college golf program. He made an instant impact upon his arrival on campus and in team practice sessions, so much so that he was either a medalist or among the leaders through the Cowboys' 1969-70 season. He earned Honorable Mention All-America recognition, yet his success was dampened in a season-ending episode he will explain later.

✦ ✦ ✦ ✦ ✦

FIVE YEARS REMOVED from his first time hitting practice balls on an Edmond athletic field, Danny was selected one of 10 best amateur golfers in the country and represented the United States against Great Britain and Ireland in the 1973 Walker Cup. He finished as his team's lone unbeaten player.

A week later, Danny competed in the U.S. Amateur at Inverness Club in Toledo, Ohio. It was the final stop of his amateur career, including being a three-time All-American at Oklahoma State.

Because the Walker Cup was up against the PGA Tour Qualifying School dates, Danny had to choose. He opted to spend a year prior to qualifying for the PGA Tour by playing mini-tours and later the Asian Golf Tour—a harrowing travel experience that few individuals, let alone golf professionals, could manage nor endure.

Danny emerged from the 1974 PGA Tour Qualifying School having earned his Tour card for the '75 season. From a beginning pool of some 450 players, Danny, Roger Maltbie, and Fuzzy Zoeller became PGA Tour winners and lasted on Tour an entire career.

Danny shares tales about those he competed against from 1975 to 1988, his seasons on the Tour. We are there as he walks the fairway with Arnold Palmer on his rookie Tour debut, and as he plays late on an April afternoon in 1986 at Augusta National Golf Club, two groups ahead of Jack Nicklaus's historic victory march.

It all helps shape our understanding of what the Tour was like—more than a decade before the coming of Tiger Woods and increased purses—and how difficult it was to make a living playing professional golf.

✦ ✦ ✦ ✦ ✦

IN 1977, DANNY HAD AN EPIPHANY that expanded his love of racing. It happened while playing in the IVB-Philadelphia Classic at Whitemarsh Valley Country Club. It's a story that takes its own turn as if pinned to a racetrack, as Danny establishes a friendship with Roger Penske, "The Captain," one of this country's most enduring entrepreneurs in automotive history.

Danny and Roger shared many different rides together—in jets, in cars, and on golf carts. Danny helps us understand how The Captain was a great multitasker in business and earned the respect and love of his staff and employees.

The friendship between the two men would move past golf partnerships in the Bing Crosby Pro-Am in Pebble Beach to collaborate on one of this country's unique charitable events, the Michigan 500 Pro-Celebrity Golf Classic benefiting Foote Hospital of Jackson, Michigan. You can almost hear the laughter around the table and the priceless stories told in the renovated farmhouse on the property where Penske hosted cookouts for the visiting golfers.

Danny continued to seamlessly mix golf with his passion for speed, winning two Midwest Division National Championships, in the highly competitive Formula Ford class, in 1984 and '85.

He was at home with a powerful machine beneath his feet as he was rifling an iron approach from a tight lie to a target on a manicured green. Danny drove as a member of two teams—a Mustang LX for Kaufmann Racing in the World Challenge Series—formerly the Escort Endurance series—and a Sports 2,000 Swift for the Pfeiffer-Ridge team of Sonoma in the American City Racing League.

In 1985, he began Executive Golf Outings, a first-class corporate golf school company with two outings a year. It became a four-day golf school that grew to 18 annual outings with clients that included the Penske Corporation, Ford Motor Company, Worthington Steel, Toyota, Hertz and Mazda. That special gig lasted 20 years.

It didn't merit an entry in the *Guinness Book of World Records* or a *Jeopardy!* bonus question, but it was remarkable that Edmond, a town that didn't have a golf course when Danny was growing up, produced not one, but two PGA Tour professionals from the same family.

David Edwards, five years younger than Danny, paved his own impressive path to golf.

In the fall of 1980, David's second year on tour, he and Danny won the Walt Disney World National Team Championship. They finished 35-under-par that weekend, capped by a bogey on the final hole, their only miscue of the week. It annoyed them all the way to the award ceremony.

The Edwards brothers also shared a love for cars and racing, and you'll learn more about where that took them, and how David—who found his groove with motorcycles—also earned a pilot's license while attending Oklahoma State. David would follow his father's passion for flying, and piloting his father's small plane and ultimately owning two planes of his own at the height of his Tour career.

After playing 14 years full-time on the PGA Tour—never losing his exempt status, competing in 36 major championships and winning 20 worldwide professional tournaments, including five PGA Tour events along with the Japanese Taiheiyo Masters—Danny left the Tour.

He founded Royal Grip Inc. and began manufacturing golf grips. While it was a shocking decision for a fully-exempt player to make, it was evidence of Danny being true to himself and assessing where he was with his life and golf. He admits in these pages that he knew he didn't have the game to win major championships. At closer glance, his putting acumen was lacking when it mattered most.

Becoming a business entrepreneur is one thing, but Danny worked to make Royal Grip a game-changer in a market dominated by Golf Pride. You will learn how his painstaking research paid off as he applied some of the racing principles of rubber meeting the road in racing to developing a high-quality, longer-lasting golf grip.

He got the idea, he said, while thinking about how he qualified his race cars on soft "tacky" tires that gripped the racing surface. If one could have a "tacky" grip on a golf club that would provide a soft feel without slipping, it would be a game-changer, he mused.

Danny enlisted the help of an old friend, engineer Dennis Livesey, and their research and development hit a stride.

Royal Grip became the antidote to the hard, slippery grips that golfers used during that time. Professionals had the luxury of changing grips at any time due to equipment trailers setup on Tour sites. But Danny reasoned that the average amateur golfer didn't want to spend the money to change out grips as often as they deteriorated.

On April 16, 1990, two days before the start of the Kmart Greater Greensboro Open, Danny stepped onto the practice range carrying two cases of grips. Life would never be the same.

Royal Grip grew to $15 million in sales in five years and earned Danny the title of 1994 Entrepreneur of the Year for manufacturing in Arizona.

A successful initial public offering followed before Royal Grip merged with Precision Shaft Company. Things were progressing well with support from PGA Tour professionals, amateur golfers and golf club manufacturers. It was time for the company to spread its wings.

You will hear from Danny on the remarkable and emotional journey of the "kingdom" of Royal Grip. Twists and turns affected the lives of its 350 employees, and an insurmountable manufacturing problem ultimately became the one hazard that Danny could not avoid.

Danny remained on the board of directors of what became Royal/Precision Inc. for two years and then returned to competitive golf and the Champions Tour (today's PGA Tour Champions) in 2001 when he turned 50 years old. He continued to compete at a high level despite having been away from tournament golf for five years.

A decade after he had taken the reins of a company that would revolutionize a vital piece of golf equipment, Danny accepted another position. It would become one of the most soul-searching periods of his life.

✦ ✦ ✦ ✦ ✦

IN 1998, Danny was asked to become president of the Tour Players Association (TPA), a group of professionals who wanted simply to make the Tour better—through financial accountability, protection of the players' interests, deferred compensation, a pension plan and transparency from leadership. Danny teamed with fellow professionals Mark Brooks and Larry Rinker to form a core that worked over a period of nearly two years to convey the group's intentions to Tour management and its members.

The problem was that Tour leaders, and some notable players, believed such a movement was an insurrection, an attempt to topple the foundation of professional golf in this country. In truth, the TPA was really a bold and difficult step, which led to improving communication channels within the Tour.

From joining the PGA Tour Champions at age 50, to developing The Chipping Equation in 2019, Danny has never been one to remain long in one place. He is justifiably one of this country's best and unsung short game expert coaches. He is engaging and popular with students of all abilities. Anyone signing up for a session with Danny comes away enlightened and a touch more exuberant about that next round of golf.

The quest to enjoy the open road in our lives is an ongoing mission not only for Danny but perhaps all of us. As a young man behind the wheel of a sports car, he admittedly pushed the limits of exhilaration and speed on our nation's highways. Danny shares stories that could inspire a new version of the *People's Court* television series.

Danny estimates he's driven between Oklahoma City and Los Angeles at least 10 times, non-stop. That 18-hour stretch on I-40 West touches four states. On those drives, Danny has had plenty of time to think about where he's been in life and what he has yet to accomplish.

Often driving a red Ferrari that would make any auto lover drool, Danny would slow down as he reached the outskirts of the City of Angels before dawn. The horizon would be shimmering like a bed of stars. When I hear him talk about those journeys, I am reminded of his remarkable life story, a Renaissance man even as he marks 70 years.

Los Angeles was once home to Coach John Wooden, who guided UCLA to 10 basketball championships. Wooden and Danny Edwards, who loved basketball, never met. But it's not a stretch to equate the two gentlemen's respective inner drives for self-improvement.

Wooden, the Wizard of Westwood, was once asked the definition of success:

> *"Peace of mind attained only through self-satisfaction in knowing you made the effort to do the best of which you're capable."*

Danny Edwards never let a challenge stymie his dreams; he always worked the problem.

—**BOB DENNEY**

CHAPTER ONE

HANGING WITH THE CAPTAIN

Friendship and a Singular Charitable Event

✦ ✦ ✦ ✦ ✦

It's 1977. I'm in my third season on the PGA Tour, and I'm playing in the IVB-Philadelphia Golf Classic at Whitemarsh Valley Country Club in Lafayette Hill, Pennsylvania. The tournament, sponsored by Industrial Valley Bank, enjoyed a great run through 1980.

It's after a Tuesday practice round, and I'm about to stumble upon one of those special moments in life when you feel the stars aligned and things I never thought possible are ready to happen.

A few of us guys were sitting in the locker room talking about cars—Bruce Lietzke, George Cadle, Bill Rogers, and maybe a couple others. Roger Penske, the renowned race car team owner and businessman extraordinaire, had listed several of his IROC Camaros for sale in *Autoweek* magazine.

The cars were identical, except for the paint colors, and had been driven by 10 or 12 professional drivers in the IROC, International Race of Champions. The drivers were from different countries and several professional racing series, such as Formula One, Indy Car, NASCAR and so forth.

I said to George, "One of those IROC Camaros would look pretty sweet in your garage."

"Edwards," he said, "you are the one who should own one of those beasts!"

Bruce chimed in, "Edwards, you should call Penske and buy one. I'll get his phone number for you."

I thought, "Why not?" After Lietzke found the number, the others watched as I used the locker room phone.

A nice lady answered, "Is Mr. Penske available?" I asked.

"May I tell him who's calling?"

"Danny Edwards, PGA golf professional." She put me on hold for about 10 or 15 seconds.

"Hello, this is Roger Penske."

I about choked, then managed to say: "Hello, Mr. Penske, this is Danny Edwards, I'm a PGA Golf Professional and we're playing in the IVB Philadelphia Golf Classic. I saw your ad selling several of your IROC Camaros. I wanted to make you an offer on one and we wondered what the price tag on a couple of those would be?" (Bruce had said he might be interested in one as well.)

I told Mr. Penske about my interest in racing and that my buddies here also liked racing. We dickered a bit. "Well, what's your offer?" he asked.

"$6,000," I said.

Roger chuckled, "Well, we aren't at the same price there. But, how about if you guys come up here to the race shop tomorrow and I'll give you a tour?

I was ecstatic. I hung up the phone and told the guys that we had an invitation to Roger Penske's race shop. They looked at me like we had inherited a gold mine.

We practiced early the next day then headed up to Reading to Penske Racing.

Roger was fantastic, giving us a grand tour around the race shop and introducing us to some of his employees and crew members. They even asked us for autographs.

"I recall when Danny and I first met in Reading, although I never did sell him that IROC car," Roger said. "I've always enjoyed golf and so to meet and connect with a group of PGA Professionals who also were car and motorsports buffs was an opportunity I could not pass. So, I asked them to come to our shop for a visit."

After the tour, Roger invited me to his office. He said, "Danny, do you play in the Bing Crosby tournament?"

"Yes, I do, and I love Pebble Beach," I said.

He said, "Do you have a partner?" When I said no, he asked, "Would you like to play together?"

I couldn't get out "yes" fast enough.

Through my passion for cars and racing, I had watched Penske Racing teams for years and now here was Roger Penske asking if I wanted to be his partner at the Bing Crosby Clambake!

"I would love to, Mr. Penske."

"Call me Roger, please!" He added, "Have you ever been to a NASCAR race?" I had not.

"Why don't you come out to the race in Phoenix this fall and be my guest?"

Less than 24 hours ago, I had been at the golf course in Philly, shooting the breeze with my buds in the locker room. Now, I'm sitting in Roger Penske's office after touring his race shop, making plans to join him at a NASCAR race, and then partner with him in the next year's Bing Crosby Clambake.

In racing, that is called lapping the field.

✦ ✦ ✦ ✦ ✦

THE NIGHT BEFORE experiencing my first NASCAR race, I arrived at a hotel in Litchfield Park, Arizona, some 20 miles west of the airport. It was close to 10 p.m., and I didn't want to call Roger's room that late.

I told the front desk attendant my name and he immediately said, "Oh yes, Mr. Edwards, we have been expecting you. I have a note here for you from Mr. Penske."

As he handed me the note, I detected a little smile out the corner of his mouth. I opened the envelope.

"Welcome Danny.

Hope you had a good trip out to Phoenix. Call me in the morning at 7:36."

I looked up at the fellow behind the desk, who just shrugged and grinned. "Yes, that was the time he gave: 7:36."

It was my introduction to the schedule of "The Captain," alias "RP." The man who once captained winning sailboat teams carried military precision to auto racing.

My virgin NASCAR racing experience was fantastic—meeting the drivers, then standing in the pits smelling the fuel and breathing the burning rubber was unbelievable as the cars flew by only inches apart. I knew then and there that I would be doing some serious racing sometime in the future.

Watching Roger interact with his drivers and team was a thrill and the beginning of a special relationship that would last for years. Little did I know that within 10 years, I would be a two-time Midwest Division national champion in the very competitive SCCA Formula Ford class.

Pebble Beach is one of the special places on earth, with its spectacular Pacific Ocean views from an unforgettable golf course and the amazing homes on some of its borders. My first year at Pebble was the 1972 U.S. Open as an amateur, and now, four years later, I was playing in my second "Crosby."

My time there with Roger and his wife, Kathy, was very special. It included meeting their friends who were playing in the tournament and going on to cheer The Captain around Pebble and nearby Spyglass and Cypress Point.

> "I was impressed with Danny's knowledge of the game of golf and his equal passion for automobiles and racing. I don't quite remember how the topic of the Crosby tournament arose that day, but I was a huge fan of the tournament. So, I thought I'd ask Danny if we could play as partners in it. He was able to arrange it, for which I'm still grateful, because it sparked the beginning of our friendship and provided some happy, memorable times on some great courses as a result."
>
> —ROGER PENSKE

The Crosby was a chance for Roger to rub shoulders with other titans of industry and what a thrill it was to listen to some of their stories. George Coleman was there from Pennzoil with tales about "The Match"—the legendary 1956 duel at Cypress Point between the teams of Ben Hogan and Byron Nelson vs. then-amateurs Ken Venturi and E. Harvie Ward.

One afternoon at Pebble Beach in 1983, after the Sunday pairings were announced, Roger called and said, "Guess who we are playing with tomorrow."

"Who?" I asked.

"Sandy Tatum." Sandy was paired with Calvin Peete, and Roger recalled the details like it was yesterday.

"Playing with Danny when we were paired with Calvin Peete and Sandy Tatum was one of those times I'll never forget," said Roger. "I think it may have been the most nervous round of golf I ever played". In addition to his work with the USGA, Mr. Tatum was a well-respected attorney who was a golf course architect and a great promoter of the game. Playing with him, I wanted to be sure that I got everything right in terms of golf etiquette and adherence to the rules."

That night, Roger asked me for a rules tutorial and also asked to be briefed on "any other things" I would consider important when we played.

"I was determined not to embarrass Danny or myself," said Roger. "Danny graciously complied with my request and the round that next day went off beautifully, although I probably could have played better."

We had a wonderful time that Sunday. Sandy didn't call any penalties on Roger and I managed to finish fourth in the tournament.

There was more to savor than golf with Roger during our early years playing together. Following a practice round and lunch one day, Roger invited me to join him for a ride to the airport. We got into his private jet, and when the wheels went up I asked, "Where are we going?"

"Just wanted to stop in at a couple truck rental locations and see how they are doing," he said.

I was privileged to enjoy these impromptu visits more than once. Roger would call a facility on the plane's phone: "Hey, I want to stop by and see how we're doing. I'll be there in 15 to 20 minutes."

He would look at me with a grin and say, "There's probably some hustling going on down there now!" We would swoop in, meet the main guys, tour the facility and grounds, and then head back to the airport to go see another location.

The facilities were always spotless, even in the service and repair areas. There was not a piece of litter or a cigarette butt to be found on a five-acre property.

It was the same at Roger's facility in Reading. You could eat off the floors.

✦ ✦ ✦ ✦ ✦

THE ONE AND ONLY MICHIGAN 500 PRO-CELEBRITY

AFTER A FEW YEARS partnering with Roger in Pebble Beach, I suggested that he ought to have his own charity pro-am golf tournament. It could be staged near one of the racetracks he owned and raise money for a local charity. He said, "That's a great idea! You put it together."

With Roger's encouragement, I called Gene Haskett, president of Michigan International Speedway, and shared my ideas. Away we went. Gene was a fantastic guy and we worked together for years on the Michigan 500 Pro-Celebrity Golf Classic, which benefited Foote Hospital in Jackson, Michigan.

A native of tiny Switz City, Indiana, Gene went to Western Kentucky University on a basketball scholarship. After graduation, he taught and coached basketball for three years. He then ran an insurance agency.

Gene's love for Indy Car racing began at age nine, when he saw his first Indy 500. That kicked off his amazing streak of attending 62 editions of the "Greatest Spectacle in Racing" through 2021.

Gene sold his insurance agency and headed to Cleveland to follow his passion. In the early 1980s, he became vice president and general manager of the Budweiser Cleveland Grand Prix at Burke Lakefront Airport where he met Roger Penske there and later led negotiations to sell the event to The Captain in 1985.

Roger then asked Gene to take over the Michigan International Speedway, and added, "There's a golf tournament there. We're not making a penny, and every year we write a check for $50,000 for the hospital. I want you to turn this golf tournament into something real, where it's making a profit that we can give to the hospital."

From 1984 through 2000, we were able to donate all net proceeds from sales of amateur playing spots and sponsor fees to the hospital—more than $1 million.

I began asking players for commitments, and each year brought between 15 and 18 Tour professionals to the event. That number crested at 36 after Gene stepped in and managed the commitment process which included meeting the players at the Doral Eastern Open in Miami.

Among the entrants over the years were Bob Gilder, Doug Tewell, Jeff Sluman, Tom Purtzer, Bob Tway, Robert Gamez and Carl Paulson. Greg Norman came every other year. We also got Don Johnson of *Miami Vice* and singer Vince Gill, a fine amateur golfer.

When Gene and his right-hand man, Barry Gibson, visited Doral each year to confirm attendees for the Pro-Celebrity, they would be besieged by agents wanting to get new players into the tournament. The momentum carried to the point where we sold out our banquet tables.

Beginning in 1987, we offered each winner what was easily the most unique and coveted non-major trophy in golf. Roger commissioned an artist who was employed by Goodyear Tire and Rubber to create a gold-plated 1/24 replica of that year's winning Indy 500 race car, complete with all its sponsor markings.

According to Gene, each trophy cost between $22,000 and $24,000. Attendees at the event dinner each year would pass by that beautiful trophy resting on a stand with a burgundy velvet base and protected under Plexiglas.

Bill Kratzert won that dazzling gold-plated car one year, and about six years later, he won again. Gene recalled to me: "I was in the locker room and said to Roger, 'We have a problem. We said that no one could win the car a second time.' "

Roger didn't hesitate, "Take off your Rolex and give it to Billy and tell him we'll send him his own." Billy ended up getting a Rolex Presidential watch.

The Sunday before the 1993 Pro-Celebrity, Greg Norman captured his second Open Championship. Gene said, "OK, we won't be getting Greg Norman."

A day later, Gene's secretary radioed him that he had an international call.

Norman was on the other end. He said, "Gene, what time am I supposed to be there tomorrow?"

Gene said, "10 a.m."

"OK, I'm bringing a friend, Nigel Mansel," said Norman. Mansell was the 1992 Formula World Champion and was also the reigning CART Indy Car World Series champion. "The only problem is that he has to play with me," said Norman.

We had a "blind" draw party the night before the Pro-Celebrity, and someone had to be taken out of the foursome to accommodate Greg and Nigel. We got through it and things worked out well.

"Greg's coming to the event two days after winning the British Open was unbelievable," said Walt Czarnecki, executive vice president of Penske Corporation. "He made a commitment to Danny, and he made a commitment to us. I didn't expect him to be there, but he was. I didn't know Greg before that, but he went up 80 notches because he was a person of commitment."

Gene Haskett said the players were amazed by the local turnout. "They said, 'Gene, we play before more people here than we do on a Friday at a Tour event.' "

"The Michigan 500 Pro-Celebrity Golf Classic was put together to elevate the public profile of the Michigan 500 throughout southeast Michigan," said Roger, " as well as to further engage the citizens of Jackson in support of Michigan International Speedway, which brought so much economic benefit to the community. The whole thing was truly a win-win. The community benefited, and both the amateur and professional participants had a great time. It was fun for sure, but it was Danny's commitment and enthusiasm that made it work and kept it together."

✦ ✦ ✦ ✦ ✦

IT HAPPENED AT THE MIS DRIVERS SCHOOL

AFTER A FEW YEARS OF THE PRO-CELEBRITY, I had another pitch for Roger, emphasizing that most of the golfers like cars and followed Penske Racing. "What about staging a drivers school before the pro-am," I asked. "Maybe we could get Rick Mears, Danny Sullivan and Bobby Rahal to come in as instructors?" That talented trio usually came in and played the tournament anyway.

Roger liked the idea and said, "You put it together!"

Gene and I worked out the details. Of course, Roger wanted to do it right, and so we had each golfer outfitted with a driver suit, racing gloves and a helmet with their name painted on the side. The guys went nuts!

Those same IROC Camaros that first attracted me to Penske Racing in Reading, Pennsylvania years before were now part of what drew a group of PGA Tour winners to the Irish Hills near Jackson to run laps around the two-mile Michigan International Speedway (MIS) oval and raise money for a great hospital.

One of the biggest fans of our Michigan 500 Pro-Celebrity was Bruce Lietzke. He was one of the first players to sign up for the drivers school and couldn't wait to participate. But Bruce was quite a conservative guy on the racetrack as we lapped with the Camaros and Dodge Chargers.

We kidded Bruce when he spun out over in Turn 3, hitting the wall, that he wasn't going fast enough to even scratch the car. Bruce always joked that you could move the MIS 500 event opposite The Masters and he would still come to the racetrack.

"It was a thank-you to the players for their support and to generate funds,." said Walt Czarnecki, whose office today is still adjacent to Roger Penske's. "We had to have the players there Monday and Tuesday and then go on to turn around quickly to go back to the Fedex St. Jude Classic in Memphis. Each player received $2,500 as an appearance fee and virtually all contributed that money to Foote Hospital. It was fun to watch these men enjoy themselves on a day off."

The first years of the Drivers School there were no restrictions, and a guy might want to get into a car and accelerate more than another guy. As Gene Haskett vividly recalled, "We learned a hard lesson."

There were 12 IROC cars scheduled to race the following weekend. They were staged at the end of the pit lane, bumper to bumper, two wide, six rows deep.

PGA Tour professional Ron Streck got into a car, with all the guys watching. You may remember Ron, the University of Tulsa star who earned the nickname "Milestone Man." He was the first PGA player to play with a Gary Adams-designed metal driver, and in 1981 was the first to win a Tour event with a metal driver. In 2005, with a victory in the Commerce Bank Championship, Ron became the first to win events on all three U.S.-based men's professional Tours—the PGA, and the then-Nationwide and Champions Tours.

This particular day, however, wasn't historic for Ron. Gene Haskett said to me, "Somehow, Ron got it in third gear and killed the engine. Guys were yelling, 'Hey, pop the clutch!' Well, he put it in first gear, popped the clutch, went down the track, lost control and plowed into the back of the race cars. He tore up four of them plus the one he was driving."

Everybody felt bad, because Ron was embarrassed in front of his peers. After some members of the pit crew raced down 50 yards to see if he was OK, I also went down and tried to offer some consolation.

After the mishap, Roger asked if I thought Ron should go back out in another car. I told him it was his call.

Roger said to Gene, "We gotta get him back, get him back in a car. Gene and Jay Signore—who was running the IROC series—huddled with Ron and said, "Don't get this car above 5,000 rpms! Do that and you'll be fine." Not much later, Ron was ready for a warmup lap.

"Jay and I were up on top of the pit box and had our stopwatches," Gene said. "He comes out of Turn 4 and we both look at each other and go, 'Oh, shit!' Ron goes into Turn 1, but goes way over into Turn 2 and hits the wall. So, one man in a matter of a couple hours tore up six race cars."

After the dust settled, Roger continued his tradition of inviting us to his beautiful farmhouse for a cookout.

I told Ron that he needed to show and apologize to the golfers, and to Roger and Gene. He did not want to do that, but he did come to the farmhouse and begrudgingly issue an apology.

Aside from that day, things were pretty smooth and continued to be special in the MIS 500. It was a major boost to the area.

Jackson was the home of some great golfers, including Dave and Mike Hill, who were longtime PGA Tour veterans and winners. A couple of years later, I said to Roger, "What do you think about a junior boys and girls clinic before the pro-am where the professionals can help a group of aspiring young golfers?"

Roger liked that idea but the board members didn't, citing concerns about safety and traffic. But in the end, they were persuaded that it would be a great opportunity for those young golfers.

I paired each one of my golf professionals with a junior golfer and divided the group in half. I put one group on the driving range for a half hour of full swing instruction and the other group over by the practice green for instruction on chipping and putting. Then they flipped stations.

The success we had and the comments we got from the kids and the parents was amazing! The next year, we had probably 200 attendees, including parents, neighbors and family members come out for the Junior Clinic.

Some of the memories I cherish most about the Michigan 500 Pro-Celebrity were those when professional drivers exchanged stories with the golfers. One year after the cookout, everybody had left except Roger, me, Bruce Lietzke, Rick Mears, Bobby Rahal, Danny Sullivan, Bill Rogers, and probably Bob Gilder.

I wish there had been a video camera trained on this group sitting around the kitchen table.

The racers wanted to hear the golf stories and we wanted to hear the racing stories. And Roger was there with us the whole time. It was priceless *(see box on right for a story).*

Rick Mears told a story about an Indy Car race in the late 1970s in Atlanta, when he was leading Mario Andretti with 10 laps to go.

Turn 3 on that 1.5-mile oval was right into the sun. Toward the end of the race, some drivers would put on sunglasses under their visor because the sun was so blinding.

As the race drew to an end and Rick was sweating in the car, his sunglasses slipped over his nose and blocked his right eye. Mario was right on his tail and kept getting closer.

With three laps to go, Rick could see only out of his left eye going into the third and fourth turns at approximately 180 miles per hour. To make matters worse, his helmet strap—which keeps the driver's head upright under the high-G forces going through the corners—had broken, and the only thing he could see out of his left eye was the guardrail at the top of Turn 3 and 4.

With two laps to go, he went into Turn 3 again, and the sunglasses fell completely over his nose blocking his vision. Then his neck gave out and he had to push his head up with his right shoulder so he could see.

As Rick was narrating and demonstrating this, we were falling on the floor laughing.

With one lap remaining and both drivers still running nearly 180 miles per hour, Rick went through Turns 1 and 2, still looking for Mario in his rearview mirror. Heading into Turns 3 and 4 on the final lap, he looks in his rearview mirror and he can't see Mario. He doesn't know if Mario has gone high or low to pass him.

"I just drove it right down to the bottom of the track and hung on

IN THE SUMMER OF 1985, I called Harold Arthur "Red" Poling, president of Ford Motor Company, and made a pitch. Earlier that year, I had the pleasure of playing with "Red" in one of our PGA Tour events and we had a great time.

"Red, I have an idea for a corporate golf school that major corporations could use as an entertainment and incentive program," I said.

"That sounds interesting," said Red. "It could be a good opportunity for Ford to show our appreciation to dealers for their hard work".

I founded Executive Golf Outings in 1985, and through 2005 it was a very special gig at locations ranging from La Quinta, California, to Pebble Beach, and Pinehurst and TPC Sawgrass in Ponte Vedra, Florida.

I'll never forget a final night in La Quinta. Dan Kaplan, president of Hertz Equipment Rental, planned to announce a price increase to his guests, who were his customers in the heavy equipment business. Dan had wanted to announce the increase at the beginning of the event, but I had persuaded him to wait until the last evening.

Dan was brief, thanking everyone for coming and adding that he hoped they had a great time. Then he dropped the price increase right on them, and the room went deathly silent.

It seemed like an eternity until a big guy, who must have been one of the toughest customers in the group, stood and said, "Well, I'll tell you one damn thing, Kaplan, this is the nicest thing you have ever done for us, and as far as I'm concerned, as long as you bring us back to this event, you can raise your prices every year."

The place erupted. Guys were high-fiving, shouting, and raising their glasses. The mariachi band at the back of the room swung into action, and it became a magical moment for me and the terrific staff at Executive Golf Outings.

for dear life," said Mears. "I went across the finish line and won the race!"

Rick said, "I got in the pits and got out of the car and everybody is congratulating me for winning. Nobody knew I couldn't see anything going through 3 and 4 on the last two laps. The crew was shouting "what a fantastic job I did holding off Mario Andretti," he said.

"I sat there on the pit wall for 15 minutes and then here came Mario. He said to me, 'Mears, you son of a bitch, you are one hell of a driver!' I didn't have the heart to tell him that I had done it almost blind!"

> **"I would say that Danny's passion for auto racing to this day—I don't know if it's equivalent to what it is for golf, but it's not far behind. Danny had been an SCCA champion.**
>
> **He enjoyed driving. He understood the cars. I think that sets him apart from a lot of people who participate. He understood the cars mechanically, just like he understands the mechanics of golf. And that passion hasn't abated him in any way.**
>
> **He understands the sport, the discipline. He had more fun at the Michigan 500 Player Days than anything. You couldn't get him out of the race car."**
>
> ***—WALT CZARNECKI, EXECUTIVE VICE PRESIDENT***
> ***PENSKE CORPORATION***

The Michigan 500 Pro-Celebrity Golf Classic was a success, and Walt Czarnecki says it begins with Roger Penske's upbringing.

Walt, a native of Detroit, has been friends with Roger for over 50 years. They met in the late 1960s when Roger was running Penske Racing Group and Walt was with American Motors.

"It goes back to the way Roger was raised," said Walt. "He was from Cleveland, Ohio, and I knew his parents. He had a wonderful mother and father who always encouraged him to achieve. They were not overbearing, but he had the right psychological makeup to accept it.

"When he accepted a challenge, no matter what it was—business, automotive, or golf—he wanted to be the best. He did what he needed to do to be the best. That's one of Roger's really great attributes.

"There was something his father told him that has become a mantra in our company—effort equals results.

"Basically, if you work hard enough, you're going to get the results. It may not always be the results you want, but you're going to get a result and you can build on it."

All things must pass, and that includes a charitable golf event. When the Michigan International Speedway was sold in 2000 to International Speedway Corporation, the new owners decided to discontinue the golf tournament.

✦ ✦ ✦ ✦ ✦

AN UNFORGETTABLE RIDE WITH THE CAPTAIN

IN THE 1980s, after we had played in several Crosby tournaments together, Roger invited me to his 25-acre property in Red Bank, New Jersey. During this time, I joined him on a trip to Detroit Diesel, a plant that he had just taken over.

General Motors decided it wanted to sell the assets of Detroit Diesel Allison's diesel engine operations in 1988 and the Penske Corporation was the successful bidder.

Said Roger, "It had seen better days."

Over the previous seven or eight years, Detroit Diesel's market share had dramatically declined through what Roger described as "a series of technical miscues."

"The product was not competitive and employee morale was dismal," he said. "There was a lot for Detroit Diesel to do to get back to its previous position as the industry leader in the on-highway diesel engine business.

Through the efforts of a talented and motivated team of people over the next several years the turnaround did occur on several fronts.

"But none more meaningful than the employee part."

When I arrived to meet Roger, I remember that the inside of the plant appeared to have not been painted for years. Half the massive diesel dynamometers—devices for measuring the torque and rotational speed (RPM) of an engine, motor or other rotating prime mover—were broken or not operational.

The plant spanned at least a million square feet under one roof. There were lanes with stoplights to handle the cart and vehicle traffic. We drove from the corporate offices directly into the plant, just Roger and me in a golf cart.

It was noisy in there with the machines running, and the workers were wearing earplugs. We were not even 50 yards inside when people began to recognize Roger as the driver and started clapping and cheering.

As we drove slowly, workers came out from behind the massive presses with wide grins on their faces, giving high-fives like they were cheering for a champion.

It became a parade. Workers were patting Roger on the shoulders, reaching to shake his hand. Some pulled out pencils and paper to get his autograph.

At first, I thought it was really bizarre. Then Roger turned to me and said, "Danny, last night, every one of these men and women in this plant got a bonus check in their mailbox for the first time in five years."

The futures of these workers—and of their children—had been

going down the toilet with Detroit Diesel. This man, Roger Penske, was like the Pied Piper to them. He had resurrected their lives, and their families now had a chance. It was a seminal moment for them.

Roger was like a general getting the troops ready for battle. It was like he was the workers' candidate and had won.

"It was a lifeboat for those employees, because they didn't know what was going to happen," said Walt Czarnecki. "There was a reason for them to come to work. It became a good place to go to work. Many of the same managers were there with the start of Detroit Diesel and they were there for the rebirth.

"We employ more than 60,000 people globally. We utilize the term —human capital—and Roger took that very seriously. One of the first things he did was to work hard to address all the grievances. He made a rule at one point. Nobody, that is, the union management or our corporate management went home on a Friday night until a grievance filed that week was resolved that night."

"When we came in, there were more than 2,000 open grievances that the union had filed against the company," said Walt. "The number of grievances dropped to virtually none after a few years.

"But the process took time," said Roger. "People worked hard and smart. Everyone had to buy into a shared vision for the future if we were to succeed—and they did."

"By the time we sold the business, 20 years later," said Walt, "it had become an American model for management and labor relations —and by the way, with the same workforce."

My trip to Detroit Diesel was one of the most emotional experiences of my life. It was my chance to witness Roger's leadership and his remarkable business acumen up close.

"When we were finally in a position to reward the employees for their efforts we were obliged to do so," said Roger. "They deserved it. I am so glad that Danny was able to experience that special moment with me as we rode through the plant together."

Those experiences would become even more meaningful when I took the leap into founding my own business and when I later was thrust into the arena as president of an association that would make its own unique history.

It all goes back to a golf cart ride with The Captain.

CHAPTER TWO

PROUD TO BE AN OKIE FROM EDMOND

No Limits in Pursuit of Being the Best

✦ ✦ ✦ ✦ ✦

My circuitous route to growing up in Oklahoma was a journey that would make any student of the history of the Land Run proud.

It began with my birth in Ketchikan, Alaska. Three months later, after my mother learned of a tuberculosis scare among the Native Americans, we moved to Kansas City.

My dad, who served in World War II in the Air Corps as an air traffic controller and meteorologist, was a weather forecaster and manager at the airport in Ketchikan. He joined us in Kansas City six months later and started a cabinet making business. He also worked in sales with a local radio station. My sister, Anita, was born in Kansas City.

From there, we moved to Neosho in southwest Missouri, where my father found a new career path working for a lawn and garden equipment company. That was where I attended the first three grades of elementary school and where my brother, David, was born.

My father partnered with a guy in Missouri, and their lawn and garden equipment venture picked up to the point that we moved in

1960 to Edmond, Oklahoma, some 14 miles north of Oklahoma City. Dad had expanded his sales territory to include Oklahoma and Texas. I was nine years old and ready to start fourth grade.

Dad later sold his part of the company and became a business instructor at the University of Central Oklahoma.

You could find us at First Baptist Church every Sunday morning and evening from as early as I can remember through high school. That's 10 years of perfect attendance and I have the pins to prove it. Mom, Anita and I even were part-time janitors for the church.

We lived by Christian principles and the Golden Rule was a family credo. My parents taught me that a "job worth doing is worth doing right."

From my early days, I was a guy interested in sports—baseball, basketball, but golf was nowhere in my vocabulary. I lived in a town that didn't have a golf course or driving range, and nobody I knew played golf.

I loved to compete. Whether it was skipping rocks across a pond to see who could go the furthest or climbing a tree to see who could reach the highest perch, I was game.

I didn't look at myself as a great athlete or a future professional. Not in my wildest dreams. It was simply a love for sports and for the competition that sports provided.

My basketball and baseball career began in the first and second grade. My mother would take me to the junior high basketball court so I could practice and play with the guys. That was my life.

Another one of my loves was riding my bicycle and, of course I wanted to be the fastest rider. I wanted to jump across a creek, or spin around trees or go over a hill. I don't remember all the things I did, but I never got hurt. Well, once I crashed while flying around a downhill right-hand corner on my paper route, but that was it.

My first job was delivering the *Edmond Sun*, and I would gather the papers left outside my home before daylight, roll them up and put a rubber band around each paper, stuff them into a canvas bag, drape the bag across the handlebars of my Schwinn Sting-Ray, and off I would go in the dark.

I made a sport of it, trying to land each paper beneath the customer's front door. I got good at staying on my bike and throwing the paper 20, 30, maybe 40 yards from the street and having it land right up on the porch.

Mowing yards—oh, how I made that an art form, too. With my dad in the lawn and garden equipment business, I knew about the equipment he sold. During the summer, I made money mowing two or three yards a day. I'd get $5 for a big yard and $3 for an average yard. Edging would get me another buck. I could do three or four yards on a good weekend.

I wanted to be the best that I could be at what I did. I busted my tail to mow yards with precision and edge them perfectly. I wanted the accolades of the people whose yards I mowed. I wanted to hear them say, "Wow, that Danny Edwards, he mows the yard beautifully!"

I didn't get that kind of support from my dad. I didn't know it at the time, but I probably compensated for that lack of support by concentrating full bore on whatever job I was doing.

It was like that in basketball, too, where I wanted to be the best. I wanted the approval of my coaches.

Before basketball practice we would run a three-mile loop around the high school. Twenty, 30, even 40 of us would run twice a week. And I won every race.

When we worked on our legs by running stairs, I was the first one up to the top and back down for three years in high school. I stood 5-foot-11 and weighed about 140 or 145. I wasn't a big kid, but I could run like the wind.

I went out for football in junior high, but I didn't like it because of all the equipment I had to wear. It felt like armor, like I was carrying someone on my back and I couldn't run as fast as I normally could. That was what really put me off about football. We had these big clunky shoes with ridiculous old big spikes.

I went back to the basketball court and practiced, getting ready for the season.

I have no idea why I was so driven to excel in sports. I was a good student, making the State Honor Society and the National Honor Society. Grades were important. But my focus was on the baseball field, the basketball court. When golf season started, I was thinking about hitting those balls.

✦ ✦ ✦ ✦ ✦

I WAS PRETTY MUCH ALONE through those early years, playing hard to get support and encouragement from my coaches and other parents. I learned fast, was observant and worked hard.

My inner drive may have come from my mother, Donna Mae McCandless. Mom was a great teacher and loved children. She grew up on a farm 16 miles outside Kingfisher, Oklahoma. She graduated from high school at age 16 and three years later, in 1947, received her undergraduate degree in early childhood education from Oklahoma A&M. She later completed her master's degree in 1963.

Mom taught first grade for seven years before being hired by Central State University in Edmond. She later headed the college's home economics department for a couple years.

My father was a friendly man, and quite different from my mother, particularly in regard to his children. To Frank Todd Edwards Jr., we were loud and rambunctious. He wanted peace and quiet. He would retire to the living room each evening, close the door, and read and listen to music.

Dad had no interest in sports of any kind. We never played catch or shot baskets, never watched sports on TV. He would occasionally attend my high school basketball games, but he'd bring books or magazines to read while sitting in the stands.

One day a hot rod came speeding by the house when we were taking out the trash. Dad was mad when I hollered out the name of that muscle car.

"Cars are a childish whim you will soon forget," he said. I have never forgotten that comment. He couldn't have been more out of touch with me.

I've always been close to my sister, Anita, who is 21 months younger than me. She was a cheerleader in high school and supported me at all the sporting events and in some very special moments. She would often get up early to help me roll those *Edmond Sun* papers before I headed out on my route. If I was sick or had to be at an early meeting at school, she and Mom would finish the route for me.

Anita would go on in life to impact and enrich the lives of so many children. She opened a preschool with Mom as her partner, and also raised a family.

One day Anita revealed that my dad had "a really bad taste in his mouth about sports" because of his dad."

My father had been born in Fort Smith, Arkansas, the oldest of five children. His father was a school administrator and coach, an abusive man with a bad temper.

They were a poor family of seven—Grandpa, Grandma and five children—during the Great Depression. My father went to school barefoot. He would hide his only toy behind the garage so no one would touch it or take it while he was gone.

Grandpa and Grandma would leave Dad from time to time to supervise the younger kids of the family. If they returned home and saw something broken or learned someone had done something wrong, Grandpa would take it out on my dad.

Due to the hard life of the Depression and my grandfather's temperament, it was hard for him to keep a school job for long. I didn't really get to know my grandparents, as they moved west and were not a part of our lives.

My grandmother did leave us with one indelible statement, which Anita shared: That "education is the way out of poverty."

When I came along loving sports, it was at odds with my father's hard upbringing and beliefs. As I mentioned earlier, my father had served in the Air Corps in World War II. He later bought a small airplane.

One day Dad's love for flying resulted in a near tragedy that turned into a modern-day version of the Keystone Cops.

Dad was at a small-town airport in Oklahoma showing off his Mooney M-18 Mite, a single-engine monoplane that was marketed to fighter pilots returning from the war. First introduced in 1947, it featured low wings and a retractable tricycle-type undercarriage.

A few guys were with Dad on the tarmac, not far from the terminal, as he started the plane.

Some single-engine planes start only if you prime the propeller by hand before you get in and hit the starter. You have to be sure the starter is turned off before you prime it.

This time the starter wasn't turned off, and the engine fired. It was a stroke of luck that Dad wasn't killed. He jumped out of the way, as did the other guys. The plane started rolling out on the tarmac under its own power.

As the plane sped up, Dad and his entourage jumped into a fire truck and chased it.

At the end of the tarmac was a little hill, and as the fire truck came closer the plane turned itself around on the hill and headed back toward the terminal. The men made a spinning turn in the fire truck with the plane on their tail and raced ahead.

Just as my dad and the guys were frantically wondering how to protect the terminal and anyone around them, the plane hit a ditch, made a sharp right turn, and smashed into one of the hangars.

Not long after that I received a call from my dad. He got a flatbed trailer and we drove from Edmond to the little airport. I got busy picking up the pieces of the Mooney Mite and loading them onto the trailer. We strapped everything down and hauled it back to Edmond.

I didn't get to practice my golf that weekend.

I'm sure that psychologists could explain what effect it has on a son when his father is not interested in his interests or his chosen career. I only know that my father was a good man, and he was engaging with people and had a respectful personality.

While we didn't have a father-son relationship where we shared our passions, he did imprint upon me the value of treating others with respect. I always believed that I inherited from him the ability to make friends, to make people believe that I was trustworthy.

On my mother's side, her drive to excel came from a family of pioneers. Her parents made the second Oklahoma Land Run in 1890, when my grandmother was 3½ months old. Louis Calavan, who was our mother's grandfather, staked the family's claim in Kingfisher County.

About the same time, my paternal grandfather Tom McCandless made the Land Run, registered at the county seat and faced a big problem with his stake in the ground. He rode 13 miles back to the property and found a "squatter" who wouldn't leave and demanded $50 to depart. So, my great-grandfather paid him. It was all the money he had.

Faced with few options, great-grandfather McCandless decided to return to Kansas and work the harvest for three months while his wife and infant daughter remained on their property. He built a dugout with a lean-to roof for them and left on horseback. It's hard to imagine.

My mother attended a little country school in Omega, Oklahoma. The boys in the school overran the teachers, and her father didn't feel Mom was getting a good education. She moved in with her Calavan grandparents in Kingfisher, where she had the chance for a better education.

Everyone liked my mother, and I never heard a single negative thing uttered about her. She excelled on so many levels growing up, becoming the best teacher, the best Sunday School teacher and the best mom anywhere. She wasn't a disciplinarian, and didn't need to be, because if we misbehaved, she would just say that we had disappointed her. That was enough.

While a teacher with the home economics department at Central State College (today's University of Central Oklahoma), mom established a laboratory preschool program to train college students. Soon there was a waiting list for children to be enrolled in the program.

After the preschool program that my sister Anita started was up and running, Mom left the college and started a daycare center. It was so highly regarded that teachers and administrators from across the state would visit to learn from her.

As busy as she was, Mom found time for her children. Over the years she attended many golf tournaments, often with Anita, to support David and me. When David qualified for the PGA Tour, she often would walk 18 holes in the morning and another 18 in the afternoon on days when we had opposite starting times.

My mother, the amazing woman who spirited me out of Alaska at the right time, continued to work after retirement for her friends, Chuck and Betty Bowman, truly great people, at the Fellowship of Christian Athletes. Chuck was the state director of FCA, and Mom was the office receptionist through 2015, before her health began to decline. She passed away in 2018.

✦ ✦ ✦ ✦ ✦

I'M NOT SURE WHERE and when my love for competition began. In grade school, I was a popular kid because of my performance on the baseball and basketball teams. Of course, I had to be a good student because my mother was a teacher, but my athletic skills and winning attitude seemed to draw classmates to me.

Before I played golf, I would spend hours throwing a baseball against our outside basement wall and catching it. I imagined I was a Major League shortstop turning a double play in a big game.

At about 13 or 14 years old, I got permission to attach a basketball hoop to the edge of the roof of our house. I cleared and leveled the ground and shot baskets at night.

We celebrated "Olympic Week" in Mrs. Hurt's sixth-grade class at Clegern Elementary School with events for both boys and girls. Each student could only pick three events, so I competed in two foot races of different lengths and the softball throw. I won both my races easily and threw the softball 30 yards farther than the second-place boy did. The girls made crowns out of leaves for the winners, and I carried home three.

In junior high, which encompassed the seventh and eighth grades in Edmond, I played trumpet in the band as well as baseball and basketball. We had good teams, and I started every game both years, playing shortstop in baseball and guard in basketball. My good friend Eddie Wilkens was the other starting guard, and we could both shoot. Coach Robinson was tough and yelled a lot, but not at me. We won a lot of games in those two years.

Aside from sports, I loved to spend time outdoors—throwing rocks at trees to improve my accuracy, riding my bike, hiking in the woods, climbing trees. I was a bit of a daredevil, not stupid, but confident in any activity that called for athleticism and coordination.

At one spot deep in the woods a pipe crossed a creek bed, probably 30 to 40 feet above the ground and spanning about 100 feet. All I needed to hear from my buddies was that they had never seen anyone walk across that pipe. Of course, I had to cross it and I did, with no problem.

Edmond High School, founded in 1893, was renamed Edmond Memorial High School in 1975 in honor of six alumni who perished while serving in Vietnam.

There were nearly 300 students in each grade during my years there. I looked forward to school. I had many friends, respected my teachers and coaches, and went about my business never getting in any trouble.

My studies were important to me. I made the National Honor Society each year and was selected as one of four seniors to represent our school at Boys State, sponsored by the American Legion. Boys State remains among the most respected and selective programs of government instruction for high school students in the U.S.

As captain of the varsity basketball team my senior season, I was responsible for escorting the homecoming queen to center court, placing a crown on her head, and giving her a kiss.

The queen was Sharon Little, and I was more worried about that kiss than about winning the game. The only kisses I was used to were pecks on my mom's cheek. There I was at center court with this beautiful girl, sweaty from just finishing the first half of the game and with packed grandstands on both sides.

I put the crown on her head, and as I leaned in to kiss her, she opened her mouth so wide that she could have swallowed my lips and nose! I almost recoiled in shock and couldn't get back to the locker room fast enough.

Through high school, I was too busy with classes, basketball, and golf to do much dating. My weekends were spent hitting golf balls at a park or a sports field because there was no golf course or driving range in town. I'd drive around in my beat-up 1962 red Volkswagen convertible, find a promising spot, look to see if anyone was around, dump some balls on the ground from my shag bag, and start hitting. I could practice for hours, but sometimes I only got a few minutes in before someone appeared and said that I couldn't hit golf balls there.

Although I was selected to the All-State High School Basketball Team my senior year, I was focused on golf. A few junior colleges and small colleges recruited me for basketball and offered a small scholarship, but I knew that my future, if there was to be one as a professional athlete, was in golf.

Toward the end of my senior year, I was selected Mr. Edmond High School by the student body, an honor recognizing excellence in academics, citizenship and athletics. I had to do a ceremony with Miss Edmond High School, Hayden Abney. I was a little more prepared for that kiss, but not much.

By the time I reached high school, my basketball skills and work ethic elevated me to become one of the best players and highest scorers on our teams. The sophomores, juniors and seniors were practicing in the same building, so I was competing with the best players of all three grades.

I made the varsity team as a sophomore, but Coach Clester Harrington wanted me to get the experience playing, so I would start and play on the sophomore team and an hour later change into the varsity uniform and come off the bench. I don't remember if I started any varsity games that sophomore year but I got plenty of minutes.

The varsity basketball team traveled to a Thanksgiving tournament that fall and Coach Harrington had me and one other sophomore make the trip. Of course, we had to carry the other guys' bags and shoes and sleep on the floor while the juniors and seniors slept in beds.

I told Mom about that when I got back home and she couldn't believe it. She said, "That's not right! You were a sophomore who made the varsity team. You were an upcoming star. They should have been carrying your bags and shoes."

"Mom, it doesn't work like that!"

Edmond High School was a Class 3A school, one division below the large 4A schools in nearby Oklahoma City. We played those schools often, and the competition helped when we faced our area 3A opponents. Our team was pretty good my junior year and we made it to the state tournament at the Oklahoma City Fairgrounds.

We reached the semifinals on Saturday evening to face Clinton and the Bell brothers who later played football at the University of Oklahoma. I drew the assignment of guarding Roy Bell, who at 6-foot-2 and 210 pounds, was a bull to cover with my 5-foot-11, 140-pound frame. We lost a close game but had a fun experience playing before 5,000 people.

The Oklahoma City Fairgrounds was a special place for basketball in those days. During my sophomore year, I went to the Christmas All-College tournament, which featured Louisiana State University's legendary "Pistol Pete" Maravich along with several other great teams. A few buddies and I sat through all three games LSU played.

Pistol Pete had something like 53 points in the first game, 56 in the second, and 54 in the finale against Duquesne University. He drained bombs toward the end of the championship game. The noise was so loud, it felt like the roof was going to blow off the arena.

During my senior season we had lost four seniors from the previous year's team, and I was the lone returning starter. Our tallest player was 6-foot-3 center Tom Conklin, and our only chance was "small ball."

Although we didn't have the height to compete at a high level, it was a fun season with my running mate, guard Billy Mike Thompson.

Ralph Bullard, our varsity coach, mentored me and Billy Mike. Coach was special in another way, too, because we all went to the First Baptist Church and shared the same beliefs on and off the court.

Coach Bullard had 10 children—eight boys and two girls, who were the bookends of the first-born and the last.

Coach had played guard in college and knew that Billy Mike and I were going to work hard and do whatever it took to win. Billy Mike called Coach a blessing to us. Like my father, Billy Mike's dad wasn't involved in sports.

Billy Mike was a very good athlete and we played well together. Most teams we played used a box-and-one against us. That meant one defender on each corner of the lane and one player guarding me wherever I went, so there were always two guys guarding me.

Those were the days of eight-minute quarters and no 3-point line. I still managed to average 20 points per game and make the All-State team.

One night we played Del City, one of the big Class 4A Oklahoma City teams, on their home court. The crowd was wild and having a real laugh because our "big" man, Tom Conklin, was out sick and at 5-foot-11 I was our tallest player on the court. They played a box-and-one defense, but I was hot that night and had 21 points, enough to lead to a 61-50 victory.

We probably didn't get two rebounds that whole game and had to slither out of the gym for fear we were going to get the crap beat out of us by that crowd.

A few weeks later, I managed to score all 28 first-half points against Guthrie, a 3A rival that always had a good team and won state championships in 1968 and '69. We were able to beat them a couple times.

Billy Mike paid me the highest compliment. "Danny wasn't afraid of the big shot at the right time. He never got excited and never got mad. He just worked harder."

As of this writing, I still hold our high school's single-game scoring record of 41 points, a record that has stood for more than 53 years. It happened in my senior year on February 11, 1969, on the road against Crooked Oak of Oklahoma City. The previous mark was 38 points, shared by Jon Keirns (1965) and Perry Snead (1966).

That night, we were so far ahead that Coach Bullard pulled me out midway through the fourth quarter. I was sitting on the bench when one of my Edmond friends behind us in the bleachers hollered, "Edwards! Edwards! You got 39 points, and the school record is 40. Tell Bullard to put you back in so you can get the record!"

I moved down to sit by Coach Bullard on the bench and said, "Hey Coach, I have 39 points and Jack Risdon says that the school record is 40. Can I go back in and get the record?" Actually, Jack didn't realize that I already had the record by a point.

Coach said, "All right, go in!"

I remember taking a shot from outside today's 3-point line that missed. But I did find the basket on another long distance shot, and that was enough for Coach to pull me out. We rolled, 92-46.

Billy Mike and I were teammates from Little League baseball through sophomore year. I played shortstop and Billy Mike was our center fielder. He ended up signing with the University of Central Oklahoma, where they offered him a joint baseball and basketball scholarship. He tried both sports his freshman season, then devoted the rest of his college career to baseball, where he was a center fielder and leadoff hitter.

When my golf career took off, Billy Mike caddied for me a number of times. He said it best: "We are the kind of friends that even if we don't see each other for a long time, when we do, we pick up as if we see each other every day."

It was Billy Mike who heard it straight from me when I made a life-changing decision during my sophomore year, "I'm not going to play baseball this summer," I said. "I'm going to learn to play golf."

"You're out of your mind," he said.

✦ ✦ ✦ ✦ ✦

MY DAD SOLD LAWN and garden equipment for Wheel Horse, and one of his clients was Guthrie Country Club, a little nine-hole course about 10 miles north of Edmond on I-35. Dad would drop me off at the club so I could play and practice.

Soon my buddy, Paul Walters became my driver to the course. Paul was six months older than me, and after he earned his driver's license his junior year we rode in his first car, a Chevrolet Corvair.

Corvairs had gotten a bad reputation from Ralph Nader's 1965 book *Unsafe at Any Speed*. Well, the Corvair worked just fine for Paul and me on our way to and from the country club, where his father and mine had each purchased us junior golf memberships.

We eventually met a couple players from Guthrie High School, including Artie Nelson. Artie would bring another of his friends from their school team and we'd play quarter or fifty-cent matches. It was good competition, and we just enjoyed pretty much living on the course in the summer.

Edmond High School was one of 260 secondary schools in the United States—eight in Oklahoma—with a bulldog as its official mascot. The bulldog is admired for its tenacity; and while I wasn't consciously thinking of mimicking a mascot, I was relentless in my pursuit to be the best. I would stay in the gym shooting baskets until they told me to go home, and I'd remain on the course practicing until sunset.

Billy Mike said that the bulldog characterization works for me because "Danny decided to do something, such as shoot a basketball or learn to play golf, he went at it full force."

"Actually, he was more of a wolf: calculating, developing a plan, working on the plan and executing it to perfection."

Being an Edmond Bulldog shadowed me all the way to Burkburnett, Texas, where our family spent Christmas 1966 at my Uncle Reid's home. Burkburnett High School also has a bulldog as its mascot.

That Christmas afternoon, with Dad strolling like a one-man gallery, I shot a 43 on my first-ever nine holes of golf on Burkburnett Municipal Course. I didn't realize it at the time, but I had become a golfing bulldog.

CHAPTER THREE

BRIGHT LIGHTS, BROTHER DAVID, AND IT HAPPENED ON TOUR

Earning a PGA Tour Card and Unforgettable Moments

✦ ✦ ✦ ✦ ✦

Don't let anyone tell you that making a living playing golf is easier than other sports. Becoming a Tour professional is an endless walk through a gauntlet without a safety net.

When I began my path to the Tour, there were three first-stage qualifying locations. I chose the East Coast site, which was in the Carolinas. There were nearly 150 hopeful qualifiers at each of the three locations, with the low 25 players from each site advancing to the National Qualifying Tournament in California.

The grass on the greens at the course I was at were gone! Peter Oosterhuis won the qualifier, I was second and we advanced on to the final where there would be about 100 guys for an unspecified number of spots. The exact number would be nailed down when we all got to California.

We were scheduled to play four rounds at the Silverado Resort and then finish in Palm Springs with another four rounds at The Canyon Club. One of my three sponsors, Paul Creasey, had a place at Silverado and let me stay there for the tournament. Paul came to support me during the qualifier. Unfortunately, I lost a golf ball on the very first hole he ever saw me play.

My faith and solid background were anchors in the face of numerous obstacles that can get young players off track. I was fortunate to have that solid direction.

The challenge of making it on the PGA Tour is to finish as one of 15 or 20 players out of 400 to 500 each year to survive Q-School. There was Monday qualifying, with 150 players to get one of 15 or so spots into the tournament, then beating half the field to make the cut, which included all the exempt players, tournament winners, and major champions.

Pressure would start to build up if a player missed a few Monday qualifiers in a row or a few cuts because he wasn't making any money.

If you could advance to the Tour, then the challenge was making enough money to finish in the top 60 money winners at the end of the year, or winning a tournament to gain exempt status.

My first PGA Tour event was the Phoenix Open at Phoenix Country Club in early January of 1975. The weather was perfect.

The locker room attendant knew my name and showed me to my own locker. I open it and see three dozen brand-new Titleist golf balls and three new golf gloves. In a side room was a beautiful buffet lunch for the players only. This was amazing!

My practice rounds were good and I was feeling on top of the world. This was what I had dreamed of for the past four or five years as I watched these guys on TV accepting their trophies. I was finally here, starting my journey to the winner's circle.

My rounds on Thursday and Friday were good enough to make

the cut, and who did I get paired with on Saturday, but Arnold Palmer and Frank Beard! Two weeks before, I had been in Edmond, hanging out at Kickingbird Golf Course chatting with PGA Head Professional Art Proctor and the boys. Now, I had qualified for the tournament and made the cut in my first PGA Tour event and was playing with The King in the third round of the Phoenix Open.

The crowds were so large we could hardly get over to the practice range and to the first tee. It was a zoo and the only people rooting for Frank and me were his wife and our two caddies.

On the par-5 seventh hole, Arnold's and my second shots ended up a foot apart on some bare hard pan, hole high, to the right of the green. It took forever to get all the gallery back far enough for us to play. Arnold's ball was about a foot outside of mine, so he was first to play after I marked my ball. We had about 10 yards to carry a bunker and then only five steps or so to the hole.

We had very little green to work with. I figured if I clipped the ball just right it would skip past the hole 10 feet. Arnold hitched his pants up and surveyed the situation several times. He caught the ball a little thin so it raced past the hole and barely stopped on the far fringe of the green 40 feet away. The gallery oohed and awed.

I stepped up and with my young nerves, clipped the ball perfectly, just carrying the bunker landing perfectly in the collar. The ball checked and stopped three feet right behind the hole. Other than Mrs. Beard and our two caddies, maybe 10 people put their hands together.

I walked up on the green feeling pretty good about my shot, marked my ball, careful not to step in Arnold's line for fear the fans might start throwing things at me, and sidled back over where Mr. Beard had been standing all this time.

As Arnold was getting ready to roll his putt. Frank leaned over and said softly in my ear, "Son, very few young men can play that shot. Well done!" Thank you, Frank. Actually, that wasn't exactly what he said, but let's just go with what I can print.

By the end of the year, I had made 27 cuts out of the 33 tournaments I entered and finished the year 80th on the PGA Tour money list with $27,000 in official earnings. That sum was no fortune by today's standards, but additional money from pro-ams, outings, and international tournaments raised my total revenue to $80,000 for the year, not a bad sum in 1975 for my first year as a 24-year- old rookie.

✦ ✦ ✦ ✦ ✦

I'M PROUD TO SAY that my brother, David, followed me to the PGA Tour and paved his own path to success.

David has said that we have "a complicated relationship in some ways. We have a lot of the same interests, but a different temperament and motivation. Danny being five years older, it was a point of contention."

I was five years older and hell-bent on making my mark in the world. I was running in fifth gear while David ran in first. He was slow, deliberate, a plodder. There's nothing wrong with that. I was running to get to the top in everything I did, and there's nothing wrong with that, either.

My mother was adamant about taking him with me when I went to practice. That was OK. But David dragged his feet most of the time. He was either picking at a piece of grass or distracted by something else.

Our dad took David with him to a few fly-ins to meet other airplane enthusiasts. David got his pilot's license while attending Oklahoma State, and he flew my dad's plane for a while. After establishing himself on the Tour, David purchased a plane of his own and flew until 2011.

David shared my love for cars and racing, but he preferred minibikes and motorcycles. His wife, Jonnie, joined him on a Harley motorcycle for longer rides. They had two daughters: Rachel, who is married and living in Hawaii, and Abby, who perished in an automobile accident in 2014.

"I was competing against what he had accomplished to get to where I wanted to go," said David, "but it was where I wanted to go.

"Danny likes accomplishment and he likes the attention, and that's comfortable, not in a bad way," he said. "I enjoy having success, but I don't crave attention. I used to say that I would love to finish second 10 times on the Tour and never win a tournament and I would be perfectly happy. Standing up to give a speech is not particularly comfortable for me."

David had one advantage that I didn't when I got started in golf. In May 1971, two years after I graduated from high school, the city of Edmond got a golf course. The Floyd Farley-designed Kickingbird Golf Course opened just 15 minutes north of downtown Oklahoma City.

David was about 12 years old when he began playing golf. He said, "I played because Danny, who is five years older, played. That's all there was to it. All I did when I was growing up was tag along. I did whatever he did. He was the one who encouraged me to get a set of clubs."

In the ninth grade, David got a job at Kickingbird as a "range rat" picking up golf balls and sweeping floors. He could play all he wanted in between work. Art Proctor helped David with his swing.

"Danny and I didn't come from a golf background," said David. "We didn't know what a Vardon Grip was or a swing plane. It was more watching. I learned to be more competitive and work hard and focus and concentrate by watching Danny than learning how to swing a club.

"I didn't necessarily feel like I was following him. It certainly appears that way and, in essence, it's like riding in the wake of a boat. The water is a little smoother and the direction he went made it easier on me by far.

"I had a pretty good gauge of how he had done, and when I came through I could tell how I was doing. It was a benchmark to go by. It opened doors for me along the way that he didn't have the benefit of."

David enjoyed his share of success during his career, but he admitted it wasn't easy. "At every level—from juniors, through high school, then college and the Tour—I had to start at the bottom and work my way up. I wasn't an instant success."

He did make his mark by winning the Oklahoma State Junior Championship in 1973, and the 1978 National Collegiate championship for Oklahoma State. He was a two-time All-America selection before turning professional in 1978.

He enjoyed his own unique career, winning five times on the Tour, including the 2009 3M Championship as a member of the PGA Tour Champions. David's major championship record includes sharing third in the 1984 Masters, tying for 11th in the 1993 U.S. Open, tying for 14th in the 1987 PGA Championship, and tying for 46th in the 1994 Open Championship.

When David returned home from his great performance in the 1984 Masters, my sister and her family took him out to dinner. "Someone came up to the table to congratulate David on a good tournament," Anita recalled. "After that person left, our boys asked, 'David, don't you wish you'd won The Masters?"

David said, "No, not really. Because if I did, I wouldn't be able to do this with you all. If I'd won, people would be coming up to bother me and I couldn't be myself."

She added: "He once told me that if he could make a living at golf so that he could do the other things he really liked to do, he'd be happy."

David went on to win the 1993 MCI Heritage Golf Classic at Hilton Head Island, South Carolina on his 37th birthday. As he strolled to the 18th green, the fans sang "Happy Birthday" to him.

Neither of us will ever forget the fall of 1980, David's second year on tour. We carried the brother relationship to the ultimate, winning the Walt Disney World National Team Championship. We finished 35-under-par that weekend.

But we bogeyed the final hole. It made both of us mad even though we won.

"Golf is a team sport in high school and college to a great degree, and you see your teammates often in tournaments in the summer," said David. "You get on the tour and it's a little lonelier. To be able to play with my brother was extra special, more so than a friend. We set our strategy early. He liked hitting first and I liked hitting second. It fits our personalities.

"We didn't come from a golfing family, and we didn't have a golf course in Edmond until I was in the ninth grade. It's pretty amazing that you'd get two brothers on Tour out of that concoction. But that's the way it ended up."

✦ ✦ ✦ ✦ ✦

PLAYERS IN SPORTS inevitably have disagreements. However, in golf, the gentleman's game, those disagreements can make players and spectators more than a little uncomfortable during competition.

During my PGA Tour rookie season, I was playing in the Canadian Open at the beautiful Royal Montreal Golf Club. Gary Player and Tom Watson were at odds during this time over the issue of tapping down spike marks. During Saturday's third round, all three of us were playing well, and I was paired with these two chilly competitors.

No sooner had we walked off the first green than Tom's caddie Bruce Edwards, no relation to me, came jogging up, clubs rattling: "We saw Gary tap down a spike mark, did you see it? Tom is livid."

I was just trying not to step in these two major champions' lines on the green. Eagle-eying whether Gary was tapping down a spike mark was the furthest thing from my mind.

The friction started building. There was no conversation between the two for the rest of the round, just icy stares.

There was a long par-4 on the back side of this great course with a pond in front of the green and deep rough on both sides of the narrow fairway. Gary drove in the left rough, Tom drove in the right rough and I hit the middle of the fairway. We're all about the same distance off the tee waiting for the green to clear. Gary was over by his ball on my left taking full practice swings with an iron sending massive wads of grass into the air, somewhere near his hidden ball. Across the fairway, Tom stood looking over at Gary with his arms crossed and breathing fire from his nostrils.

As the green cleared, Gary replaced the iron with a fairway wood and proceeded to knock the ball some 200 yards over the pond and onto the green. Tom was watching Gary's every move like a hawk, then finally gouged his ball out of the thick rough up short of the pond.

We finished the round and entered the scoring tent, where Gary sat in the left chair, Tom in the right and me in the middle. You could cut the friction with a knife. Not a word was said. I had Tom's card. Tom had Gary's card and Gary had mine.

Abruptly, Tom stood up and spoke to the scorer in our group, "I will not be signing Mr. Player's card." He pivoted and walked out of the tent. I signed my card and handed it to the scorer as Gary sat there silently.

Everyone was looking around like, "what do we do?" Finally, someone radioed Jack Tuthill, the PGA Tour tournament director, to come to the tent.

"What is happening here?" asked Tuthill, the cool, former FBI agent who was an equal parts enforcer, psychiatrist, and comforting friend to pro golfers.

The scorer said, "Mr. Watson said he will not sign Mr. Player's scorecard."

Jack looked at me and at Gary, then picked up Gary's scorecard and signed it. As he turned to walk out of the tent, he said, "We cannot have an international incident here."

As far as I know, no stories about the episode appeared in the next morning's sports sections and things ended there.

✦ ✦ ✦ ✦ ✦

WHEN I WON my first tournament on Tour, the 1977 Greater Greensboro Open, I celebrated over dinner that night with Butch Leal, a professional drag racer who lived near Greensboro.

Butch had been introduced to me by my uncle, Jim McFarland, in California. We ended up playing golf quite a few times.

Earlier that day, I played the final round with George Burns and Larry Nelson. I don't remember anything out of the ordinary, except George hit a ball out of bounds over the eighth green. I made a great birdie on 18, using a driver and a 6-iron to about 10 to 15 feet.

We had the presentation ceremony on the 18th green. I will never forget the official saying loudly to the crowd, "And, he gets a check for $47,000!" It was a big check in those days—bigger than what any major champion took home that season. It is more like last-place money on the Tour today.

That win kicked me up into the top 60 money winners and I was exempt for the remainder of that year and the next.

After winning at Greensboro, I was going to The Masters the next week. That was wonderful, of course, but I had other plans I needed to address.

I was planning to race, to run my Formula Ford in the Hallett Motor Racing circuit outside of Tulsa. I had to let Ed Branch — my right-hand man, my mechanic, my tire changer and fueler — know what was going on. Ed was a big ol' guy, weighing about 280 pounds, who had played football at the University of Central Oklahoma. He reminded me of Grizzly Adams. Ed and I had started a little business buying and selling sports cars. We sold a half dozen cars over a period of a few years.

Ed and I enjoyed having fun with people who visited our garage, which was by a racetrack. I would whisper to him, "Ed do your thing."

He went over and lifted the back end of a race car with his bare hands.

When I phoned Ed from Greensboro that Sunday, I told him I was going to The Masters. He said, "What's that?"

✦ ✦ ✦ ✦ ✦

IN 1981, I WAS COMPETING in my third Taiheiyo Masters in Japan and playing well. The golf course was very well-maintained and tree-lined with beautiful Mt. Fuji as a backdrop. Tom Watson and Jumbo Ozaki were in my final round pairing.

My caddie was a young Japanese boy who spoke no English, but that was fine. I could tell he was more nervous than I was. It was nip and tuck all day, and standing in the fairway on the 16th, a tough long par-4, I was leading by one shot.

The pin was on the back left of the green on a slightly elevated plateau. I thought to myself, this is the kind of shot that can win you a tournament. I stood 198 yards from the hole. It was just a good 3-iron for me. I made a good swing and when I looked up the ball was flying straight toward the hole.

It stopped three feet from the flagstick and I made the putt for a two-shot lead with two holes to play, a par-3 and a par-5. We all parred the 17th, and so I had a two-shot lead standing on the 18th tee with a very tight driving tee shot coming up. For many years I carried a 1-iron and that was the club I had already decided to tee off with if I had a lead. I striped it down the middle.

Jumbo took a wild swing and drove it into the trees on the right.

Watson played a good drive into the neck of the fairway where he could reach the green in two. I laid up with a 7-iron to give myself the yardage I wanted to have for my third shot.

Tom played a fairway wood just short of the green. Jumbo was out of it. I stuffed my sand wedge in three feet from the hole, and Tom hit a good pitch to about three feet. Tom made his putt and I made mine also for birdie and the two-shot victory.

The three of us shook hands and then my caddie jumped up on me with a big bear hug and wrapped his legs around my waist. Tears were streaming down his face. And he wouldn't let go. I walked off the green with him still hanging on.

Another memory from Japan had a different ending.

I played the *Golf Digest* Tournament on a course that was literally on the side of a mountain, with Mount Fuji in the background. It was so hilly that the caddies had to hook their carts to a track in the cart paths that would pull them up the slopes and keep them from running away downhill.

The greens were a type of Bermuda grass that was incredibly grainy making it impossible to get uphill putts to the hole, at least for me.

Coming to the 18th hole, I was 1-under-par and wanted to finish with at least a par. My second shot on the long straight uphill par-4 came up 30 feet short.

My caddie, a woman, gave me the putter and then went over to the cart path to hook the cart to the track. I thought, OK, don't leave this putt short. Get it to the hole! The putt came up three feet short. I missed the second and I was hot. I probably had four three-putts in that round.

I signed my card and caught the escalator up to the clubhouse. It was the first time I'd ever taken an escalator on a golf course. I was still disgusted when I got to the top, where my agent, my caddie, and the tournament director were waiting for me.

I went over and said hello, and then my caddie said something to the tournament director. He then says to me in English, "Your caddie has advice for you!"

"OK , what advice does she have for me?"

"She says you need to hit harder on uphill putts!"

I could only laugh.

✦ ✦ ✦ ✦ ✦

"MR. EDWARDS, MEET JUDY"

I EARNED FOUR TRIPS to the MONY Tournament of Champions at La Costa Country Club in Carlsbad, California — 1977, '82, '84 and '86. My April 1982 came two weeks after I won my second Greater Greensboro Open. I'll never forget that week when I tied for sixth place among all those champions.

La Costa Country Club was developed in the late 1960s, and was one of the top luxury resorts of its time. It boasted not only a great golf course, but an equestrian center.

With the walkway between the green and the tee roped off, golfers are really just a thin line away from the fans.

Early in the first round that week, I was walking through and happened to glance to my right. There was a very lovely lady with dark hair and a beautiful tan, wearing a white jumpsuit.

"Hello, Danny," she said as I passed by.

"Hello, how are you?" I smiled and walked on.

The next hole, she was standing by the entrance to the tee again.

"How are you today?"

"Just fine, how are you?"

I walked on and that was it. After the round, I was sitting in the locker room when the manager walked over.

"Mr. Edwards, there's a lady upstairs who would like to meet you. I'm sure that you would like to meet her."

That didn't often happen to me. I thanked him and went back to what I was doing. About five minutes later, the same manager came back and looked nervous.

"Mr. Edwards, I don't want to bother you, but I feel that you would enjoy meeting this lady."

"All right, give me a minute." I walked upstairs to the lobby, which overlooked the golf course. It was packed. The line leading into the bar and grille was long.

The moment I got to the lobby level, a maitre'd dressed in a tuxedo walked up to me and said, "Mr. Edwards, can I show you to your table?

I was thinking, what in the world is going on here? I was ushered in ahead of all those people waiting. As we approached the table, I saw the woman who had greeted me on the golf course sitting there.

"Mr. Edwards, may I introduce you to Judy Roen?"

We chatted for a while, then she asked, "Would you like to join my family and me for dinner tonight?"

I accepted. Not long afterward, I ran into a couple guys and mentioned what had happened.

The guys said, "Do you know who you met? She's the daughter of Allard Roen, and her father and his partner are linked to the mob. Watch yourself!"

They were teasing, but as a boy from Oklahoma whose only

encounter with the law had been some speeding tickets, I was naive about who this family was.

That night I met Judy at the restaurant. We were ushered to a table where I met her father and his wife, who looked like she could have been a showgirl taking a break from performing at the Flamingo. Moe Dallitz, one of Mr. Roen's partners in Paradise Development, and another business partner also were there.

The six of us had a lovely dinner then said our goodbyes. I went on and finished with a 68 on Sunday afternoon.

That was just after I had bought a Ferrari Daytona. The subject had come up at dinner, and Judy had asked if she could go for a ride.

We had a fun day driving up and down I-5. Two weeks later we met in New Orleans for the USF&G Classic.

We went out to dinner one night in a restaurant in a tower downtown. We had hardly got off the elevator when the maitre'd was there to give us the best VIP treatment.

That week, while we were driving around, Judy suddenly said to me, "You know, we could have a wonderful life together?"

I said, "What do you mean?"

"My father has $500 million, and I am the executor of his estate. We could live anywhere in the world you want to live. You can play golf anywhere, or race cars, if you want. We could have a great life together."

I learned that she ran the Frontier Hotel Casino Las Vegas and had several thousand people working for her.

I thought to myself, "Man, this is so out of my lane." I had thought that I was in the fast lane driving a Ferrari, but that wasn't even close to this fast lane. There couldn't have been two more diametrically opposed cultures riding in that Ferrari.

Judy went back to California and I went back to playing the next tournament. We stayed in touch for over a month.

Many golfers never forget details of a round. This was one of those moments, a meeting by accident, that I'll long remember.

✦ ✦ ✦ ✦ ✦

GOLF IS AN AMAZING GAME. I fell in love with it almost immediately after hitting my first golf balls when I was 14½ years old. Even today, my decision to leave the PGA Tour in the prime of my career haunts me.

The game is really four different parts: full swing, putting, short game and mental game. I did pretty well with three of the four, but putting was my Achilles' heel. My goal was always to win tournaments and a couple of majors. To accomplish that goal a player has to be a great putter; not good but great!

Putting is a completely different part of golf from ball striking. I was an outstanding ball striker and excellent around the greens. But I was never able to get to be the putter that wins majors.

My performance in 36 major championships, which included making 25 cuts, was a bittersweet story.

In my day, they didn't have the statistics that they display today. I would have been high on the list for Greens in Regulation and Strokes Gained Tee to Green. However, in Strokes Gained Putting, I would have been down near the bottom of the list.

In the majors, it was always fun to qualify, but I never could consistently get my putting to come through for me. I worked on it incessantly. I went to two Dave Pelz putting schools. I worked with Dr. Bob

Rotella for months but could not get the ball to go in the hole often enough to really win like I wanted to win.

Ultimately, that was why I left the Tour.

My seventh and final Masters Tournament was in 1986 and I was paired in Sunday's final round two groups ahead of Jack Nicklaus.

As Jack made those putts on the back nine and went on to win, the ground shook from the gallery's roars. Up ahead, we had to wait before we could play, peering back through the trees to make sure Jack wasn't getting ready to putt. The roars were deafening that afternoon among the Augusta pines. Jack had a large supply of what it takes to win majors—he was a great putter.

When you get outside of six and 10 feet, there is a lot of luck involved in putting a ball into a four-inch hole. Tiger made putts that were truly a gift from above, like the putt he made to beat Rocco Mediate in the 2008 U.S. Open at Torrey Pines.

It is a huge part of the game, and if you don't have the skill or good fortune to hole a lot of putts, you are not going to win major championships or win 20 or 30 tournaments on the Tour.

I fought it for 14 years. I tried everything known to man. Some of the best putting I did was looking at the hole, not the ball.

On October 20, 1985, I won the Pensacola Open looking at the hole. I was playing with John Mahaffey and Gil Morgan in the final round.

On the 17th hole, a nice par-3, I hit a good shot to about 20 feet right behind the hole, the ball going right over the flag. I got up there and I had a right-to-left breaker, and I read it about six inches outside the right edge.

When you look at the hole, you make your stroke and then continue to look at the hole until the ball comes into your field of vision.

That day, when I saw the ball come into my field of vision, about a third of the way to the hole, it was perfectly on the line I intended it to start. It took the break and it rolled right into the middle of the hole.

I had made the decision to start putting that way about two weeks earlier at Oak Tree Golf Club in Edmond. I was practicing over the weekend before the Texas Open in San Antonio.

My buddy, Jim Ahern, my director of golf for the Executive Golf Outings schools, was with me. I started hitting putts and making them while looking at the hole. I couldn't believe how beautifully it worked.

I putted for a couple of hours. "I'm going to the Texas Open tomorrow, and I'm going to look at the hole," I told Jim.

"I think you should," he said.

I did and I finished tied for 18th in the Texas Open. It was the first time I had looked at the hole in competition. The next week, I finished with a 66 at the Oldsmobile Classic, posting a 36 on the front and 30 on the back nine with six great birdie putts.

Afterward, my playing partner, Johnny Miller, said, "The way you putted was unbelievable! I'm going to go home and work on that tomorrow."

Two weeks later, I won the Pensacola Open and won it by a stroke while putting and looking at the hole. It was my last win on the PGA Tour. My successful putting method worked for a while, then began to fade.

I went back to conventional putting and never really caught fire again.

CHAPTER FOUR

A WONDERFUL YEAR

Earning a PGA Tour Card and Unforgettable Moments

✦ ✦ ✦ ✦ ✦

Making history never crossed my mind when I stood on the 18th tee on April 5, 1982, at Forest Oaks Country Club in Greensboro, North Carolina. I was leading the Kmart Greater Greensboro Open by a stroke and needed to par the final hole to close out my second victory in that great event.

Nearly two months later, June 6, I was at Road America in Elkhart Lake, Wisconsin—making just my second appearance in the June Sprints. I wasn't navigating through a field of more than 140 golfers, but rather 124 Formula Ford race car drivers whose intent was anything but "allow faster players through."

I went on to win, becoming the first and currently only PGA Tour professional to win a Tour event and follow it with a national racing victory.

Winning the GGO in 1982 was a totally different drama from 1977. The week's weather forecast wasn't good, and it only got worse. The biting cold mixed with heavy gusts made an already difficult Forest Oaks Country Club that much tougher.

During this time, I thought about informal gatherings we had on tour with Dr. Bob Rotella, the renowned sports psychologist from Virginia, one of the early pioneers in the field. Dr. Bob used to meet with a small group of us—perhaps six to eight players—in locker rooms, in some quiet areas of the clubhouse or in hotel rooms.

He taught us some different techniques to control our thoughts in competition and get the most out of ourselves. His strategies were quite simple but quite different from my burning desire to succeed. His strategies were simple, but they were difficult for me to get comfortable with and internalize. However, I have no doubt that his philosophies will produce better results in all types of players.

This particular April day in Greensboro was a grind, where scrambling was essential. Fortunately, my short game was my strength, and I was focused on getting the most out of it.

At Oklahoma State, I learned a chipping system for playing the ball on the ground wherever possible. As I was taught, a player has the most control over the ball when it is on the ground rolling horizontally. It made sense to me that learning a couple simple self-made formulas for carry and rollout was a much more accurate way to execute a chip with predictability.

Bobby Clampett was on my tail all day long at Forest Oaks and pushed me right up to the 18th hole. I squeaked out a one-shot victory by making a tricky three-foot par putt. That continued my string of at least one victory a year since 1980. I would go on to collect wins through 1983, miss in '84 and get another in '85.

The folks in Greensboro remain close to my heart, and owning two victories there will always be among my fondest memories on tour. When I returned to defend my title in 1983, I had conversations with the GGO tournament director and joked about wearing my race driving suit in the pro-am. North Carolina is a bonafide NASCAR hotbed. I thought it might be fun and the fans might like it.

NASCAR star Benny Parsons and I had become good friends and he thought the Greensboro fans would also love it. The tournament director was sold on the idea, so I decided to play the first hole with my suit on, then change into golf clothes.

The PING Company was sponsoring my race program and John Solheim, then the executive vice president, was on site to join my pro-am group. What a memorable team photo with four golfers and me, donned in a racing uniform with a PING helmet! I actually parred the first hole at Forest Oaks in my racing outfit.

✦ ✦ ✦ ✦ ✦

FOUNDED IN 1956, the June Sprints became the longest consecutively offered road race in the United States. It's where Indy Cars and NASCAR stock cars run annually along with many amateur races, including numerous Sports Car Club of America (SCCA) events.

My debut in the June Sprints in 1981 wasn't even worthy of a mulligan in golf. My first practice session and one of my early laps around the four-mile course, I slid off the outside of Turn 1, which was a flat, fast right-hander at around 60 to 70 miles per hour. I crashed through a fence and stopped just feet from dropping straight down a 20-foot cliff.

One year later, June 6, 1982, it became a day on a track that I wish I could bottle like fine wine. With my new Lola T540 Formula Ford, and sponsorship from the PING Company, I was ready to show 'em what I had.

I thought to myself that I had to do this the right way, and stay calm. I had the advantage of running a few laps and I knew the track fairly well. Additionally, I was coming off a season in which I won quite a few races in the SCCA Midwest Division.

I was fortunate to race in the Formula Ford Class, winning close to half the races that I entered. Our team was Performance Development and Racing out of Littleton, Colorado. We raced all across the country, from Riverside, California, to Road Atlanta, to Mid-Ohio in Lexington, an hour north of Columbus, to Elkhart Lake, Wisconsin and on.

I was ready to have a really good race.

Road racing was so much fun to me. It wasn't just getting into a car and pushing your pedal down. You had to go through so many tests in just one lap. We probably shifted 60 times a lap. You can't believe how busy you are in the cockpit, not to mention you have got 124 other cars chasing you.

In 30 to 45 minutes of road racing, you go through hundreds of moments of braking. The June Sprints were running 16 to 18 laps on Road America, a four-mile course, which is the longest road racing track in the country. Most other tracks were barely over two miles.

As the fastest car in qualifying, I won the pole position with the Lola/PING car as John Solheim, Vice President of PING at the time, watched and kept his camera clicking. One hundred twenty-five Formula Fords took the green flag and headed flat out toward Turn 1 inches apart -- all wanting to grab a spot or two before the turn.

I managed a good start and led the field through Turn 1 down into Turn 2, another fast right-hander and on to the second of the three long straightaways. The adrenaline was flowing and the pedal was jammed to the floor as we raced down through the trees, down a long sloping hill to a sharp left-hander.

The first lap is high tension as the first few rows of cars are close together for a chance to break out or sneak past a car that may only slide out of shape for a fraction of a second.

As the first two or three rows begin to separate themselves from the pack behind, the attention starts to shift to a laser focus on hitting every corner's turn-in point, hitting every shift perfectly, breaking as late as possible for each turn and making no mistakes!

Your mirrors are filled with cars, but my view straight ahead is of a clear, clean track. Hammer down!

Leading the race with three laps to go, the back markers began to show up ahead. Passing the slower cars at just the right planned spot without having to lift off the accelerator is a timing challenge. It's vital not only for safety but also my chance of winning the race.

My main nemesis, Kim Campbell, has managed to stay within four or five car lengths throughout the entire race, passing smoothly every car I passed and not losing a beat. I know I can't mess up a corner or Campbell will be on my tail and around my Lola in a flash.

The last couple of laps are like a ballet, setting the car up for each turn, hitting your turn in points, kicking the back end out and power drifting through the turn, letting the car drift out to the full edge of the track using every inch of it before getting ready for the next turn and do it all again.

Finally, the checkered flag waves and I have won the 1982 June Sprints! Qualified on the pole, led every lap, didn't make any mistakes and won a race. As I get out of the car, there's John Solheim with a handshake, my crew with hugs and the checkered flag as a winner. It was a tremendous feeling of exhilaration.

After the race was over, I was thinking there wasn't another professional golfer in the world who could do this, and no other golfer has attempted it. Some guys who win a race or a golf tournament jump up and down, holler and scream. I wasn't that kind of character.

It's a huge transition to decompress from a racing environment, where everything was loud and fast, to the peace and quiet of a golf course. In a matter of hours, I was moving from the breakneck pace of race drivers and crews to that of deliberate golfers preparing to compete against the best of their profession on a different course—complete with beautiful trees and grass, not pavement.

For over a decade, I was driving in two separate worlds. And I loved it.

CHAPTER FIVE

DIGGING IT OUT OF THE DIRT

My Fast Track to Becoming a Golfer

✦ ✦ ✦ ✦ ✦

Once a year, the Edmond High School golf team had the good fortune to play a match at either Quail Creek Golf & Country Club or Oklahoma City Golf & Country Club, the two most beautiful courses in Oklahoma City.

I thought I had died and gone on to heaven when I was playing either of those two courses.

After those matches, I would go back and drive around in my old Volkswagen and look at the beautiful homes and the golf course. I discovered in my driving around Quail Creek that the back nine was largely north of the main body of homes and clubhouse. It was like being out in the countryside.

Portland Avenue borders the west side of Quail Creek Golf and Country Club. There was a big field with waist-high grass that separates Portland Avenue from the back nine of Quail Creek.

I decided one day to jump the fence on Portland, hike across the field a quarter-mile and take a look at Quail Creek's back nine. It was late in the day, about 4 p.m., and nobody was on the back side.

I hopped over the fence and walked a couple of holes. They were absolutely beautiful.

I said to myself, I have got to find a way to play this golf course.

I hiked back, hopped the fence, walked to my Volkswagen and headed back north to Edmond. All the while, I was thinking how I am going to get on this golf course and play it. Knowing full well that if I got caught, I would probably go to jail, because the golf professional there was Ernie Vossler, a former PGA tour player, who happened to have a son, Eddie, who was my age, and played on the John Marshall High School golf team.

I had played Eddie in a couple of matches and beat him. I figured if I got caught, his dad would have me sent straight to jail for trespassing.

I contemplated this dilemma for a couple of days, and then decided it was worth the risk to sneak across that field and play Holes 11-17 out of the view from the clubhouse and pro shop. After getting enough nerve, I parked my old Volkswagen on Portland and carried my clubs across the field in waist-high grass, hopped over the fence and teed off on No. 11.

I made it to Heaven early. I visualized that I was playing a PGA Tour event, talking with my caddie, getting the yardages, measuring the direction of the wind, seeing the gallery and then playing an excellent shot into the flag. The fans were erupting in applause.

I fixed every ball mark, every divot, I made sure that every bunker was raked beautifully, and did everything that I could to take care of that golf course like it was my own.

I finished on No. 17, walked back across the 11th fairway to the fence, tossed my clubs over the fence and carried them to my car on Portland.

Driving home that first time, I was absolutely on "cloud nine." I had done it, fulfilled a dream. Nobody had seen me, I thought. I had played this beautiful golf course. So, I started to go over to Quail Creek two or three times a week. I never told a soul what I was doing.

I soon realized that the lakes and water hazards probably held golf balls, a lot of golf balls, which I needed. I didn't have the money for them.

So, one night about midnight, I parked on Portland, hiked back across the field and hopped over the fence and started wading for golf balls at Quail Creek. There were times when there was no moon to guide me, and it was pitch dark. But I knew my way around that course.

It was just unbelievable, and I did this for a couple of years.

About 15 years later, after Oklahoma State, the Open Championship, PGA Championship and The Masters, I'm playing the Bob Hope Desert Classic in Palm Springs, California.

Joe Walser Jr. and Ernie Vossler had started a company, Unique Golf Concepts, that later became Landmark Land and Development Company.

They developed a big project in La Quinta called PGA West. During one of the breaks I had in the tournament, I walked into the restaurant at PGA West and saw Joe and Ernie having lunch. Our eyes met and they waved me to join them at their table.

We talked about the tournament, the Tour, and in the back of my mind there always was my late afternoon and midnight excursions on Quail Creek Golf and Country Club. Again, I never told a soul about my exploits. But sitting there, I decided the time was right to tell Mr. Vossler that I had snuck on his golf course all those times and played the back nine and then waded for golf balls at night.

So, I said to Mr. Vossler, "You're not going to believe what I did when I was in high school at your golf course.

"What's that, Danny?" he asked.

"I used to come over late in the afternoon, park my Volkswagen on Portland Avenue and sneak across the field with my clubs and play 11 through 17, where no one could see me from the clubhouse.

He looked me in the eyes and said, "You did it two or three times a week, didn't you?"

My jaw nearly dropped, "You knew?"

"Of course, I knew."

"Why didn't you send someone to throw me off the course? I was trespassing."

"Danny, you were a good kid. You were a good player and you weren't hurting anyone. You were just working on your game and trying to get better."

I thought to myself this is the quality of PGA Professionals that we were so fortunate to have in Oklahoma City during my time growing up there.

✦ ✦ ✦ ✦ ✦

MY FIRST EXPOSURE to golf was in 1966 as I rode my bicycle near the high school football field and noticed an old man and a couple boys hitting some small white balls off the dried out Oklahoma hardpan with some kind of metal stick. I watched for a few minutes and rode home. A few days later, I saw them hitting again and the old man motioned me over and asked if I wanted to hit some golf balls.

As it turned out, that old man was E. C. Hafer, athletic director for Edmond Public Schools, and one of the most well-known coaches in the state. Edmond youth were fortunate to have had him in the community. In 1979, six years before he passed, the City of Edmond dedicated a beautiful park in his name.

Later that summer, I rode by my friend Paul Walters' home and saw him hitting those little white balls with a club on his front lawn. Paul was a teammate on the basketball team and a great student.

Paul explained that he was "chipping" balls for practice and that the game was played with holes of different lengths and with a set of clubs that sent the ball various distances.

My first experience of actually hitting golf balls on my own came after noticing Paul and then getting permission to use one of the clubs of my next door neighbor, Bill Eischeid, the local Pontiac dealer. He had a set of clubs leaning up against the corner of his garage.

Once I got that club, an 8-iron, I started hitting some balls that I had found near the high school field and used a brown paper Safeway grocery bag that I found in the kitchen. That was my first "shag bag."

Later, I searched for places to hit my bag of practice balls, moving from vacant lot to vacant lot. That became my "Ben Hogan" practice regimen. In tribute to Mr. Hogan, I was digging my game out of the dirt all over the neighborhood. Once I got the Volkswagen for transportation, I branched out all over town finding vacant lots, parks, ball fields and even a grass runway at Oklahoma Christian College!

When I got my courage up, I would occasionally hit balls over a house. This was how I worked on my game until I got my first set of clubs in Burkburnett, Texas where our family traveled to my mother's brother's home for Christmas.

My mom and dad had given my uncle $20 to find me a set of clubs at a pawn shop. Uncle Reid McCandless, who became the mayor of Burkburnett, owned a gun store in town. He found a used set of Wilson Staff Fluid Feel irons and woods in a canvas bag in a pawn shop, of all places. This was my Christmas gift for 1966, and I thought they were beautiful.

My dad and I went to the Burkburnett Municipal Golf Course on Christmas afternoon, where they offered free golf, and I played my first nine holes while he walked and watched. After finishing play, we stopped by the golf shop where the head professional asked if we had a good time and how I did.

"I did OK," I said.

"What did you shoot?"

"I had a 43."

"Well, that's pretty good. How long have you been playing?

"This is my first time ever playing on a golf course."

He looked at me like I was from Mars.

Those early months, after I got my clubs, were dominated by my basketball schedule. It wasn't until spring that I started practicing golf.

The following fall, as school began, the few guys that I had met that were on the Edmond High School golf team said, "Where were you this summer? We didn't see you at any of the summer tournaments."

"What are golf tournaments?" I asked.

In a span of three years, while living in a town that had no golf courses and in a family that had no golfers, I found my groove, a rhythm and I was on a fast track to becoming a golfer.

I also was a starting point guard on the high school basketball team. As a team player, you are relegated to the success of a team. Golf rang my bell, because I was my own man and I controlled my own destiny. That was huge for me.

I could play and practice as long as it was light. It was a very solitary beginning those first few years. I was alone in parks, old worn-out baseball or football fields hitting practice balls.

I would return home to watch golf on TV on Saturday and Sunday afternoons and watch the golf swings of professionals of the "Big Three" Era—Arnold Palmer, Jack Nicklaus and Gary Player—who were covered in earnest on TV and filled our living room viewing hours across the country.

The motion of the golf swing was imprinted in my mind from watching golf on television. As I practiced and tried to ingrain the movements of the golf swing, each motion was evaluated on whether it fit into that mental picture of the swings I had memorized from the professionals on television.

The key elements for me at this time were, keeping the ball in play, preferably in the fairway and that scoring came from inside 100 yards to the hole; distance control with wedges was critical.

The necessity for some type of system to control my distances became a major focus of my practice. I reasoned that to be a great player, I must become a great wedge player.

The importance of learning how to get the ball up and down around the greens was also a focus day in and day out. There were no putting greens or chipping greens in town, so anytime I was at a course, I spent hours around the greens practicing my chipping, playing games with myself, seeing how many balls out of 10 that I could get up and down from all around the green. Every time I went out to hit that shag bag of balls, I was alone. It was a solitary existence, but I loved it.

✦ ✦ ✦ ✦ ✦

AS A SOPHOMORE, my first season of high school golf, I was beginning to learn the Rules of Golf. In a match at Lake Hefner Golf Course, I made a 50-foot birdie putt on the par-5 10th with the flagstick in the hole. I thought I had won the hole with a birdie and felt pretty good until my opponent said, "That's a 6! It's a two-stroke penalty for hitting the flagstick while on the green."

I lost that hole with a mistake I never made again but felt good when I eventually won the match.

We had regular challenge matches among teammates on the Edmond High School team, and my sophomore year, the first year I played any competitive golf, I earned the No. 5 spot on the team. I had made the lineup for the first golf match, but was challenged for a spot in the second by Randy Granzow, a junior who beat me.

I was really crestfallen and I worked hard the following week to not let that happen again. I was ready for bear when I got the chance to challenge Randy for a spot in the third team match. I shot a 74 or 75 and he had an 85. I skunked him so bad that he never challenged me again. But, we have remained friends to this day.

Length was not a big concern in my early days in golf. I was adequate off the tee and felt that accuracy was a more important part of the game. I could tell that distance control was also an important part of this game and having that shag bag with my own flagstick to aim at when I practiced meant that I was always focused on a repeatable distance for each club.

I am basically a conservative guy and using that philosophy as a strategy in my game worked well for me. I got my scores that sophomore season below 80 regularly and occasionally were in the mid-70's. By the spring of my junior year, I was consistently scoring in the mid-70's and good rounds were getting close to par.

The overriding strategy that drove me was a burning desire to get better. My drive to win every wind sprint in basketball practice was the same desire I had to practice, practice, and more practice at golf. To me, if a player didn't have that level of desire, they were not going to get better.

I never wanted to look back and wonder if I would have worked harder, maybe I could have accomplished more.

I was gaining confidence through a number of events including winning the 1968 Oklahoma City Junior Championship at Lincoln Park in a four-hole playoff.

Meanwhile, Paul Walters Jr. and I formed a great twosome. We won the State Two-Ball Championship our junior year in Norman, beating Seminole by two strokes. Paul got me by two shots for 54 holes that day despite us both posting 80s.

My first significant amateur victory was the 1969 Oklahoma State High School Golf Championship. It was played at Lakeside Memorial Golf Course in Stillwater, the home for the Oklahoma State Cowboy golf team.

Earlier that season, Paul and I won the Oklahoma City Four-Ball Championship, which was a pretty big event with over a hundred teams competing. We beat Mark Hayes, who was the star at Oklahoma State, and his brother, Larry. Mark ended up going on to a winning PGA Tour career and Paul went on to Stanford University on a full academic scholarship.

The State Championship at Lakeside Memorial featured three different competitions—a four-man, two-man and individual divisions. Stillwater won the four-player title, while Paul and I tied Stillwater's Henry Delozier and Craig Struthers in the two-man race. We lost in a one-hole playoff.

They scheduled 36 holes of the individual championship on Monday, followed by an 18-hole finale Tuesday. When I walked up to the first tee of the opening round, the Oklahoma State University Coach, Labron Harris Sr. was standing by the markers.

Our eyes met and he said, "Danny, how are we doing today?" I was in shock. He knows my name! How can he know me? I didn't feel like a standout player. However, I was winning tournaments and playing some good golf at that time.

The imposing 6-foot-2, 225-pound and muscle-bound coaching icon then introduced himself.

"Danny, I'm Coach Harris, and I want you to come play golf at Oklahoma State University. I'm going to be gone tomorrow and won't get to see you play the last round of the tournament. But I'll get hold of you when I get back and invite you to come up here and I'll show you around. I want you to play golf for Oklahoma State."

I could have jumped beyond the rim and dunked a basketball! I shot 75 and 76 on what was a really windy day, trailing the leader by two shots on the 6,600-yard, par-70 layout.

On Tuesday, I fired a 68—the only subpar round of the tournament—and won by six shots! I wished I could have been a fly on the wall to see the look on Coach Harris' face when he learned that I shot a 68 and won the championship. Well, that was my thought at the time.

A week later, Coach Harris called. Mom and I went to Stillwater, touring the athletic dorm and the campus. Coach Harris said, "Danny, we've got a great team and players from all over the country here. If you really work hard, by the time you are a junior, you probably have a shot to make the team. I will give you a partial scholarship now, and when you make the team, I will raise you to a full scholarship."

I almost fainted. I remember like it was yesterday riding home in the car in shock with mom and thinking, what am I going to do here? Not making the team until I was a junior! I got home and thought that the only thing I can control is how hard I work, and I'll work harder than everyone else!

✦ ✦ ✦ ✦ ✦

I WAS A SENIOR IN HIGH SCHOOL when I met Art Proctor, an assistant golf professional at Lincoln Park Golf Course in Oklahoma City.

A couple years later, when I was playing at Oklahoma State, Art was PGA Head Professional at Kickingbird Golf Course in Edmond. Art and I would get together occasionally to practice. He didn't change my swing much. Art called my golf swing "natural and fluid," and because he's a great fundamentalist, he wouldn't let kids go until he had ensured that they had the fundamentals down. He said that he wanted to see what they developed on their own.

One miserable Oklahoma winter's day, Art decided that we had talked golf enough and forgo a practice session. He suggested we go play some tennis. Art had a good friend who owned an indoor tennis facility and he loaned us a couple of racquets. Art was a pretty good athlete and began hitting the ball left and right, and I would run and return the ball right back to him.

Art then hit a hard serve, which I got a racquet on and returned it straight on. This was getting fun and I loved running, so why not? Art started laughing hard and then hit one back to me, but into the net. He said that I won that "match."

Art reminded me of a time he wanted to test my strength and balance. He took eight different drivers down from a lady's lightweight flexible whip to a Double-X telephone pole men's driver and we went to the driving range.

"You couldn't flex it if you put a 10-pound ball on it," said Art. "I let you take a practice swing with each driver before hitting the ball the first time and you hit every ball dead straight! Now, if you don't think that isn't talent?"

I wasn't trying to show off, just swinging a club as I normally would. It was high praise coming from Art.

CHAPTER SIX

LEARNING GOLF THE COWBOY WAY

Growing Pains in Stillwater

✦ ✦ ✦ ✦ ✦

Arriving on campus in Stillwater the fall of my freshman year, I checked into Room 302 of Henry P. Iba Hall. Mark Hayes, the No. 1 player on the golf team, was my roommate. I doubt that happened by accident. We went to the first qualifying round at Lakeside Memorial and walked into a room where 30 to 40 guys were awaiting a tryout, most with no scholarship aid at all.

I was paired with Mark and I shot the low round of 68. I ended up making the team as a freshman and played every tournament for Oklahoma State University for four years, except the 1970 Big Eight Championship and the NCAA Tournament.

I'll get to the story about that later. It still bugs me.

One event that got me off to such a good start that freshman year was making the first hole-in-one of my life on the final hole of an early-fall qualifying round.

We had begun the round on the seventh hole of a shotgun start so that all of our groups could finish. The final hole, a par-3 sixth, was over water to a green positioned next to a dam on a lake. It was well past sunset. My ball flew right at the hole after a beautiful 6-iron shot. We heard the crack when it hit the flagstick, but we couldn't see where it had bounced.

When we got to the green the ball wasn't in sight. We looked all around, down by the water, over the green, and even on the side of the dam. Then someone said, "Maybe it's in the hole!"

And there it was, in the bottom of the cup, with a divot in the back side where the ball had hit it like a missile. That finish to a good round moved me a step closer to a spot on the Cowboy golf team.

Of all the rounds I'd played at the Lakeside Memorial Golf Course, it was unbelievable to get my first ace on the final hole of an important qualifying round for the golf team. The stars were coming into alignment for a spot on a team that Coach Harris had said I probably wouldn't make until my junior year.

That ace after dusk was the first of 26 lifetime holes-in-one through 2021, with 18 coming as a professional, 15 in competition.

The Fall Buckeye Classic was played every year at the Ohio State University Scarlet Course, where Jack Nicklaus made his mark and where the Buckeye golfers practiced.

It was the second tournament of my freshman season. We traveled nonstop from Stillwater in a Ford station wagon—five golfers, Coach Harris, all our luggage, and five sets of golf clubs stuffed into that car for 20 hours.

We arrived in Columbus around 5 a.m., and found a place close to campus for breakfast. This was in 1969, and the hippie culture was in bloom, although it had yet to invade Stillwater. Walking into the cafe we all noticed a couple tables of "longhairs," as Coach called them.

We thought Coach might turn around and leave, but hunger won out and we sat down.

The Scarlet Course was terrific, and I took to it right from the get-go. There were tall, beautiful trees and soft, manicured fairways, unlike the squat, scrub blackjack trees and rock-hard burned-out fairways of Central Oklahoma.

Many of the big collegiate teams were there. My eyes must have been locked on the Houston Cougars on the practice green, because Mark Hayes said, "What are you looking at?"

"That's the No. 1-rated collegiate team in the country."

"Get back to your practice," said Mark. "They put their pants on the same way we do."

I got off to a good start my first two rounds, and when I stood on the 18th tee of the third and final round, I saw Coach Harris walking up.

"Danny, we need a par on this last hole for a second-place team finish." That was just what a freshman didn't need to hear at that moment!

My drive found the left rough on the par-4 dogleg left hole. But I hit a good second shot that got me on the fringe of the green. I followed with a good chip and putt to save par. Our team finished runner-up, and I was third individually in the tournament and our team's low scorer.

Even in my moment of exhilaration, I wondered how Coach felt about me.

Coach Harris was a character. Born in 1908 in Dardanelle, Arkansas, he founded the golf program at Oklahoma State when it was still Oklahoma A&M. He was an all-state wrestler at Southwestern State College (today's Southwestern Oklahoma State University) in Weatherford and wrestled at 160 pounds. He also played tennis and won the

Oklahoma Collegiate Conference golf title. He graduated in 1935.

In 1947, Coach Henry "Hank" Iba hired Harris as golf coach at Oklahoma State. He went on to guide 27 All-Americans and coach the Cowboys to 24 conference titles and the 1963 NCAA Championship. Coach Harris was a great player, too, winning the 1953 Oklahoma Open and tying for 27th in the 1958 U.S. Open. He was inducted into the Golf Coaches Association of America Hall of Fame in 1980 and in 2016, into the Oklahoma Sports Hall of Fame.

Coach also taught a couple of classes, Typing 2 and Shorthand 2. I signed up for typing. I had heard he was pretty easy on the members of the golf team because we would miss class time for tournaments. But I was the only guy to sign up. He asked me to see him after class the first day.

"I don't want to see you in here again!" he said.

"What about Shorthand 2?" I asked. Coach just looked at me.

Coach was strong as a bull, but he had lost a lot of flexibility over the years. His backswing was short and consequently he didn't hit the ball very far, but when he got within 50 yards of the pin, he was deadly.

A great putter who enjoyed gambling, Coach would chip in or hole putts on the ninth green regularly to keep us players from winning "the bet" that he regularly made in practice, and collecting a new Wilson Staff golf ball from him. He got the balls for free.

One spring afternoon during my freshman season, Coach came driving out across the seventh fairway as usual to the "range," which was just a field north of the fairway.

About six of us were standing there. Coach got out of his Plymouth, slowly as usual, and asked us how we were doing. Then he said, "Edwards, see this quarter? I'm kind of thirsty. I'll bet you I can flip 10 heads in a row with this quarter. If I do, you go buy the sodas. If I can't, I'll buy the sodas."

"I'll take that bet," I said.

I was standing right beside Coach as he flipped the quarter three feet in the air, caught it between both palms, and then opened his palms to show the head facing up. Second flip, just like the first. This went on for eight more flips. Heads every time! I went to get the sodas.

A few days later, I was out hitting balls when Coach came over and said, "Edwards, you want that bet again?

"Sure, Coach. But I want tails this time!"

What were the odds now of Coach calling 20 coin flips in a row? He flipped that quarter, and each time he opened his hands it was tails. Ten straight! I marched to the pro shop for the sodas.

That night back at the dorm, Mark said, "How many times are you going to bite on Coach's bet?"

"I was standing right beside him watching like a hawk every time he flipped."

"Watch the coin closely!" Mark said.

A few days later, the same thing happened again. Coach looked at me with his sly grin and I went to get the sodas.

That night Mark said, "The coin is not turning over, it's just wobbling."

"No way," I said.

"Yes, you just can't tell!"

I later learned that Coach had spent some time with Alvin Clarence Thomas, a famed golf, gambler, and hustler better known as Titanic Thompson.

Coach had perfected some tricks, and as a freshman I was the perfect pigeon.

✦ ✦ ✦ ✦ ✦

AS SPRING ROLLED AROUND, I believed that I had secured a place on the team with my continued strong performances. I was in a solid position heading into our last two tournaments of the season, the Big Eight Championship and the NCAA tournament, which was at the Ohio State Scarlet Course, where I had played so well in the fall.

Mike Holder, the only senior on our team, was considered the heir apparent to Coach Harris. I had beaten Mike in every tournament we had played so far that spring, so I was surprised when Coach told me there was going to be a playoff with Mike to see who went to the conference championship and the NCAA tournament.

Coach told me not to worry because I was five or six strokes ahead of Mike and we were just going to play two rounds. No problem, but all the pressure was on me. After the two rounds I was still three shots ahead.

Coach said, "Let's play one more round." Mike gained just one more shot. Then Coach said we were going to play yet another round and that would be it. Mike shot a good round and got ahead by a shot. Coach said, "I've got to take Mike."

I couldn't believe it. I don't remember how Mike played at the tournaments, but he did win the Big Eight Conference individual title. I was frustrated and disappointed but just had to move on and keep working toward a good summer of amateur tournaments.

Because of a change in NCAA rules, I had become the first freshman to play for Oklahoma State, competing for the Cowboys in every other collegiate tournament that year. For my efforts I was selected Honorable Mention Collegiate All American.

By fall, I was itching to get back to the team and show Coach he had made a mistake not taking me to the conference championship and the NCAA tournament. I made a commitment to myself to play or practice every day that fall and winter, no matter the weather.

At the Tucker Invitational, hosted by New Mexico State University in Albuquerque, I finished second behind a guy named Ray Leach who I was paired with in the last round. Ray had a beautiful swing and I expected to see him on Tour someday. I was disappointed with Coach because he insisted on hitting the road home and not staying for the trophy presentation.

The NCAA tournament would be in Tucson, Arizona, the following June. I was already thinking about it, but there was a lot to do before that.

That winter my red Volkswagen was the only car in the Lakeside Memorial parking lot at least a half dozen times. The seven-mile drive out to Lakeside went by Boomer Lake. The wind is notorious in Oklahoma, and we would always check the lake as we went by to get a wave reading.

If the whitecaps were showing, that meant the wind was over 30 mph, and many of the guys would make the next left turn into a bowling alley and pass on golf for the day. Not me. It was brutal sometimes, but once we started spring qualifying I was ready mentally and physically.

After my three rounds in the 60s, I was 12 shots ahead of second place and off to a great start to the season.

At the NCAA tournament that June, I drew an unlucky tee time of 2:30 p.m. the first day. Our hotel was in downtown Tucson and Coach didn't want to drive all the way from Tucson National Golf Course into town to pick me up, so I had to go out to the course at 7 a.m. and wait all day for my time. It was so hot that afternoon, around 115, that I could only think of getting water to drink and shot 80.

I came back with a couple good scores in the low 70's to help the team, and I think we finished fourth overall.

Oklahoma State had two All-American golfers that season. Mark Hayes received First-Team All-America Honors, and I made Third-Team All-American. Knowing that my performance had put me in the top 24 collegiate golfers in the country was satisfying. I felt like I had come a long way from that guy whose high school didn't even have a golf team until his sophomore year.

My first trip to play a major summer amateur tournament was in 1971 to the Trans-Mississippi Amateur at Spyglass Hill Golf Course on California's Monterey Peninsula. The format was 36 holes medal play, qualifying for 64 championship flight spots in match play. Spyglass Hill is a long, tough course. It had the highest stroke average of any course on the PGA Tour during the Bing Crosby tournament, over 74 strokes.

I shot 73-78 and was the third low qualifier. I won my first couple matches, and then I played a little guy from Texas in the quarterfinals. The match was even after 18 holes, but I thought I might have him on the 19th hole, which was the par-5 first hole, when he bunkered his third and I stuffed my third 10 feet from the cup. I was licking my chops. He had no green to work with but hit a beautiful soft bunker shot out to a foot. I was in shock and missed my birdie putt. He won the 20th hole with a par, and I was out. By the way, that little guy was Tom Kite, Jr.!

Over the three summers of my sophomore, junior and senior years I played most of the major summer amateur tournaments across the country, staying in people's homes who had made them available for the players.

During the 1972 North and South Amateur in Pinehurst, North Carolina, I was the houseguest of veteran *Golf World* writer Dick Taylor.

That North and South brings back special memories of playing Pinehurst No. 2, the great Donald Ross creation, and facing Eddie Pearce, the defending champion from Wake Forest University, in a 36-hole final. Eddie was considered by many as the heir apparent to Jack Nicklaus, as he was a stocky kid and resembled Jack.

Along the way, I beat Curt Cox from San Antonio, Texas, 3 and 1, in the fourth round, and Rick Bendall, a University of Maryland standout, 7 and 6, in the quarterfinals. I was feeling pretty good. But then I faced another Wake Forest star, Joe Inman Jr., the 1969 North and South Champion, in the semifinals.

We had a great match, with the match dead even after I bogeyed the 17th. I hit a couple of solid shots into 18, the last an approach 12 feet from the hole. I hit that putt like I wanted, and it found the bottom of the hole.

Inman applauded with the gallery, and said later to Dick Taylor, "Sure I applaud. I appreciate good golf as well as the next guy."

The night before the championship match, I attended a cookout, where I asked nobody in particular, "How on earth do you play 16?" I had never birdied it that week. Someone suggested that I should hit a drive and two 8-irons, or "get up and bust two wood shots."

I took the latter advice, and in the morning 18-hole round, I hit two wood shots and made an eagle. I was 3-up on Eddie at that point.

I had nobody there supporting me, while Eddie had a whole cadre of his fraternity brothers and other friends. We must have had about 20 to 30 people following us that day.

The fraternity guys got a little rowdy the second half of the match, especially during the final nine. Eddie rallied to trim the deficit to one hole after seven holes in the afternoon, but I played the spoiler, going 3 up through 15 and winning the hole with a par. Eddie birdied 16 to trim the deficit to two, but at the par-3 17th, he couldn't get up and down from 12 feet and I made a 10-foot birdie to win the match.

That edition of the North and South will always hold a special place in my heart. Pinehurst is a wonderful golf destination, a step back into time.

My final two opponents that week, Joe Inman Jr. and Eddie Pearce, went on to different professional careers. Joe spent 12 solid seasons on Tour, winning the 1976 Kemper Open and sharing ninth place in the 1978 Masters. He later coached men's golf at Georgia State University.

Eddie, who left Wake Forest after his sophomore year to turn professional, had four runner-up finishes during a Tour career from 1974 to 1981. He enjoyed the party scene and never reached his full potential. He later became a success in the car sales business.

✦ ✦ ✦ ✦ ✦

MY 1972 SUMMER continued upbeat as I won the Southeastern Amateur in 1972 at the Columbus (Georgia) Country Club and had runner-up finishes in the Porter Cup, Eastern Amateur, Dixie Amateur, and Sunnehanna Amateur. I also qualified through medal competition for the 1972 United States Open at Pebble Beach Golf Links and The Open Championship at Troon in 1973, and will always cherish the warm reception from the galleries at Troon—including a standing ovation as I walked the last 100 yards to the green that final round.

Since 1960, only six golfers who have been Low Amateur in an Open Championship and gone on to win a PGA Tour event—me

(1973), Hal Sutton (1981), José María Olazábal (1985), Tiger Woods (1996), Justin Rose (1998), and Rory McIlroy (2007). Pretty fast company for a small-town kid!

I returned to the Open Championship in 1974 as a young professional, and finished tied for fifth at Royal Lytham and St. Annes, shooting rounds of 70-73-76-73. It was a fantastic experience going back to the Open after finishing as Low Amateur the previous year.

The week got off to a great start, as if by accident. As I gazed at the grandstands from the practice green, a lady asked if I was going to play a practice round. I said that I was and she introduced herself and her husband. They were from South Africa and said that their friend, Bobby Locke, was wondering if he could join us.

I had heard that name but really didn't know much about the man. He came over and shook hands as he introduced himself. He wore gray knickers, a white, long-sleeved dress shirt, with his tie tucked inside, long white socks, white shoes, and a tam o' shanter.

"Are you ready to go?" he asked, and away we went – with me not realizing I was playing with a four-time Open Champion, one of the all-time greatest putters who was just four years from being inducted into the World Golf Hall of Fame.

Mr. Locke chatted with his friends most of the time as we walked the course that day, but he was very courteous and thoughtful.

This was my first practice round for the Open Championship, so I was trying to learn the course while keeping an eye on this very interesting fellow with the unusual, hooked putting stroke. I watched his putting with interest. All his putts came rolling up to the hole with beautiful speed. It looked like a magnet was drawing them back, front, or side of the hole.

Later, I would realize what an amazing stroke of luck it had been to play a round of golf with the great Arthur D'Arcy "Bobby" Locke.

I played the final round with Lu Liang-Huan of Taiwan, a showman who distinguished himself by his great play. He would charm the galleries by doffing his porkpie hat after each successful shot, and like Chi Rodriguez, he'd put his hat over the hole after making a putt.

Mr. Lu and I shared fifth place, taking home $2,300 apiece.

✦ ✦ ✦ ✦ ✦

OF THE MORE THAN 20 local qualifying sites across the country for the 1972 United States Open at Pebble Beach Golf Links, one was at the Oklahoma City Golf and Country Club. There were usually only two or three spots available at the local qualifying sites, and I got the beautiful silver USGA medallion as the low qualifier. I had selected The Midlothian Club in South Chicago as my sectional qualifying site if I got through the local.

Midlothian was a great old course, and I went up early to get in a couple practice rounds because I really wanted to play the Open and Pebble Beach Golf Links. There were 60 players for four spots and most of those 60 guys had made it through a local qualifier so there were no slouches!

Local and sectional qualifiers were both 36 holes, a morning and an afternoon round. My morning 74 was very disappointing and I knew I had to go low in the afternoon to have a chance. Even par on the front side in the afternoon didn't give me much hope of making it. When I bogeyed the 10th hole things looked bleak.

As I walked to the 11th tee, I looked at the six or eight people watching our group and thought, not one of these people think I am going to qualify today, but I'm going to make it!

I parred the 11th and 12th holes, birdied 13, 14, 15, 16, parred 17 with an up-and-down from the bunker, and then made a sidehill 10-footer for birdie at the last for a 66 that got me a spot. I had qualified!

Two guys in t-shirts and jeans, who followed me most of the round, came up to congratulate me. One of the guys asked where I was going to stay for the Open.

Of course, I had no plans yet. He said that his folks had a house right beside the first green at Pebble Beach. "Why don't you stay with us?" he asked.

"That would be fantastic," I said. "What's your name?"

"I'm Mark Rolfing." It was the beginning of a wonderful friendship.

My dad and my brother, David, came out to Pebble to root for me and to celebrate my 21st birthday that Wednesday. What a time and place to have a birthday!

Each evening before dark, I would walk through Mark's parents' yard, go under the ropes, and putt on the No. 1 green. In Thursday's first round, I opened by holing a 30-footer for birdie. Mark, his mother, Mary, and his stepfather, Bo, cheered from their porch as I went through.

Pebble Beach was brutal for the '72 Open, with thick rough and tiny, rock-hard greens that were half the size they are today. My 77 in the first round was not bad, and was in the top half of the field.

I played with Dave Hill and Bob Murphy, two young PGA Tour pros, as was the custom for amateurs qualifying for an Open Championship. On Friday, I was again playing well through the 15th hole and was 3-over par for the day.

On No. 16, Bob and I hit our second shots to the green then waited for Dave to play his second. He pulled his shot into the trees on the left, and several marshals ran to see where it had come to rest.

Me and Bob Murphy had hit our second shots to the green and were waiting for Dave Hill to play his second. Dave pulled his second shot into the trees on the left and we watched as several marshals ran to see where it had come to rest.

When we all arrived near the area, one marshal announced that the ball was out of bounds. He should have notified Dave with a signal that that was the case, but he had not.

Dave immediately erupted in anger and started swinging and taking giant divots of rough and turf. It lasted a few minutes, with Bob and me trying to stay out of the way. He then marched back to the top of the hill on the 16th fairway to replay the shot.

It had been a shocking display, and I was distracted. Once we reached the green after the delay, I three-putted.

An unusual thing happened to me on the 17th. The pin was cut back left, and I pushed my tee shot right, ending up on the back right of the green, where I had to pitch over the bunker from the green. As I was over the ball with my sand wedge ready to play, I heard a loud, "Hold on son!"

A little shaken, I looked up to see a USGA official walking toward me. I thought, what have I done wrong? He said, "You know you should have the flagstick attended? You are on the green."

He was right, so I had my caddie go over and attend the flagstick.

Around the edges of the bunkers at Pebble was a six-inch wide band of grass that had been allowed to grow almost a foot tall. I got set up again for the shot, pitched it over the bunker, and the ball carried and went down in that collar of grass and disappeared. We looked for two or three minutes before we found it.

From there I had to take a swing like I was going to hit a 50-yard shot just to move the ball down onto the green 15 feet from the hole. My two putts left me with a double bogey 5. I didn't collect myself very well and bogeyed the 18th hole, missing the cut by two strokes.

Even so, the experience was unbelievable. Playing beside PGA Tour professionals and holding my own on a brutally difficult golf course had shown me that I could compete.

Mark Rolfing and I roomed together for five events on the European Tour the next summer while waiting to enter Q-School for the PGA Tour. I stayed in his family's home and enjoyed spending time with them—the nicest people on earth—during many of the 10 Crosby pro-ams that I played, as well as a PGA Championship and the '82 Open. Mark's career in golf broadcasting began in 1988 with NBC Sports, and he is going strong to this day.

✦ ✦ ✦ ✦ ✦

THAT PRETTY CORVETTE IN THE LOT

CARS WERE A PASSION of mine from about age 14, and it hasn't changed to this day. I learned the make, model, and year of pretty much every muscle car on the road. My mom would get so upset when she was driving and I would suddenly holler "'64 Pontiac GTO" or "'65 Chevelle SS 396" or " '63 Corvette, split window." Scared her to death, she said.

I obviously couldn't afford any of those cars, so as I drove along in my '62 Volkswagen I would imagine that it was a '65 GTO or a Roadrunner or even a Corvette, if I was really dreaming big. Years later, Ferraris became the predominant car in my dreams. I knew that somehow I would own cars like that someday.

At Oklahoma State, lunchtime in Iba Hall, which everyone called the jock dorm, was interesting. There were all kinds of looks. There were the guys who had obviously just rolled out of bed. There were the guys who were coming back from morning classes and had finally woken up. At least once a week a few wrestlers who had been out most of the night looking for fights would come dragging in. Those wrestlers were some tough dudes—tougher than the football players.

I was envious of the footballers and basketball guys because many of them drove nice muscle cars that boosters had given them or that they had bought with money they got from "cush" summer jobs that the boosters arranged.

And then there were a few golfers who earned their money in all-night poker games. Those guys rarely even went to class. Such a player was one J.R. Shade from Nebraska. After he got eligible in the fall for the spring semester, J.R. didn't go to a single class his final semester.

We golfers scheduled our classes for the morning so we could head to the course each day after lunch. I was sitting there one day chowing down when one of the athletic counselors plopped down with his food and said, "What's happening, Danny? You look like you just lost your golf clubs."

"Louie, I see all these football and basketball players with their hot rod muscle cars, and I just wish I had a ride like that. I travel all over the country in the summers playing these tournaments, bringing some attention to our university, and I'm driving an old, beat-up '62 Volkswagen.

"Why don't you go over and see our athletic director, Floyd Gass? He probably knows you."

"You gotta be kidding, " I said. "He wouldn't know me from Adam."

"I'll call him and see if he'll meet with you." Louie was gone for less than three minutes. "Go clean up and get yourself over to the arena. Mr. Gass will see you in 30 minutes. Just tell him what you told me, and maybe he can help you."

I got cleaned up and headed over to see Floyd Gass. A 19-year-old college golfer meeting with the athletic director at a Division I university. Yeah, good luck!

At the fieldhouse I found Mr. Gass's office and knocked politely. A lady opened the door. "Hello, my name is Danny Edwards, and I have an appointment to see Mr. Gass."

"Yes, Mr. Gass is looking forward to seeing you."

Really? He was looking forward to seeing me? Mr. Gass came out of his office with a smile on his face and said, "Danny, it's great to meet you! We're so proud of you and all your accomplishments on the golf course and the fine way you represent Oklahoma State University around the country."

I couldn't believe my ears. Mr. Gass invited me in, and we chatted a bit more before he asked, "What can I do for you?"

I got right to the point. "Mr. Gass, I'll be finishing my career here next year and will try to qualify for the PGA Tour. I know I'll make some money then, but I don't have any now and I'd like to have a nice car."

"What kind of car are you thinking about," he asked.

"A Corvette!'

"Are there any Corvettes for sale here in Stillwater?"

"No sir, I'll probably have to go to Oklahoma City or Tulsa."

Mr. Gass dialed the phone. "Hello, George," he said. "I've got a young man here named Danny Edwards. I'm going to send him to see you, and I want you to take care of him."

Mr. Gass wrote down a name and handed it to me. We talked for another minute or so, then he stood up, extended his hand, and wished me good luck.

In my crummy old Volkswagen I headed downtown to meet Mr. George Lucas, senior vice president of Stillwater National Bank.

"Mr. Gass says you are looking to buy a Corvette," Mr. Lucas said.

"Yes, sir."

"Do you know where you will go to look?"

"There are several lots in Oklahoma City, and if I can't find what I want there I'll go to Tulsa."

Mr. Lucas reached into his desk and brought out a large ledger checkbook. He wrote a check, signed it, tore it off, and handed it to me.

"Here's what I want you to do. Find the Corvette you want, fill out the amount on the check, call me when you make the purchase, and when you get back to town come see me."

"Yes sir." We shook hands and I walked out of the bank.

I had to tell my parents in person about my good fortune. I jumped in the Volkswagen and headed south to Edmond.

In the spring and summers in Oklahoma, the wind can really howl. As I was driving those 50 miles or so on I-35, it was like driving in the foot of water. There were times when I had to downshift from fourth gear to third in that stupid Volkswagen just to get up the hills. Totally embarrassing. I wanted to put a paper bag over my head for fear someone I knew might recognize me as they flew by. Never again, I laughed to myself.

Well, my folks weren't nearly as excited about my good fortune as I was, especially my dad. He said, "Get your butt back in that Volkswagen and take that check back to Stillwater National Bank. There have got to be some strings attached."

I said, "I don't know what kind of strings are attached, if any, but I'm not going back to Stillwater until I'm driving a Corvette!"

That didn't go over very well.

Six months earlier, I had been excited to tell my dad that I had gotten a call from a sports agent who represented Johnny Miller, Lou Graham, Sam Snead, and other athletes. Mr. Ed Barner was interested in representing me after I finished at Oklahoma State and had invited me to fly out to Los Angeles for a visit.

When I asked my dad what he thought, he was offended. He felt I had already made up my mind and that I wasn't really interested in his opinion.

The sports agent offer and now the Corvette situation were the straws that broke the camel's back as far as me and my dad were concerned. I left the house and headed for the Corvette lots in Oklahoma City alone, as usual.

Couldn't find anything I really liked at three different lots in the OKC area that sold Corvettes. I was looking for a one- or two-year-old Stingray, one previous owner, well taken care of, with low miles and no scratches. I couldn't find anything I liked at the three lots in the area.

Next, I drove to Tulsa, and that's where I found the one—a 1971 LT1 350, British racing dark green. LT1 High Performance small block 350 with white LT1 decals on the hood and 11,000 miles. There was another 'Vette with wheels I liked, so I had those wheels swapped over.

I paid $4,200 out the door and left that old Volkswagen behind as I headed back to Stillwater in my new car, feeling like a million bucks.

The next day I went to see Mr. Lucas at the bank. He asked if I thought about insurance.

No, I said. "Do you have any money for insurance?"

Well, no.

"Do you have any money if you need something repaired?"

No again.

"Here's what we're going to do. We're going to loan you $5,000 at 6 percent simple interest, renewable every six months for as long as you need. When you get out of school and start making some money you can pay it off. That's $150 every six months. Can you do that?"

I figured I could scrape up $150 somewhere every six months. "Yes!"

That Corvette and I became great friends over the next 10 years. We went to tournaments in California numerous times, with a suitcase strapped to the luggage rack on the back deck and my clubs in the passenger seat.

In the fall of 1973, I headed off in the Corvette to Nacogdoches, Texas, for my first professional tournament. My partner and friend, Bill Rogers, was an All-American and Walker Cup teammate from eastern Texas. We joined up to win the team division of the Eastern Texas Open. I also won the individual first prize, and made something like $3,500. I had won my first professional start and more money than I had ever had in my pocket.

I kept that Corvette looking beautiful, and it got a lot of good attention, including from the Highway Patrol. I tended to get a little frisky and push the needle occasionally, so I got my share of tickets.

There were no points against your license in those days, so I'd just put $5 in the envelope and send it off.

As the years went by and my taste in automobiles got much more expensive and my foot heavier, things changed significantly. Four or five years later, I would have the Corvette custom repainted and a new chromed-out motor slipped under the hood at Edelbrock under the supervision of my uncle, Jim McFarland. I also installed tucked and rolled crushed velour upholstery. I put over 100,000 miles on that beauty with never so much as a scratch on it.

On one trip coming back from Los Angeles, I stopped to get gas and stretch my legs in Gallup, New Mexico. When I came out of the store after paying, several high school guys were standing around the Corvette drooling.

We chatted for a while. I was ready to hit the road when one of the guys said, "Do you know what the girls of Gallup would do for this car?" I had a good chuckle.

Years later, having paid off the Corvette loan at Stillwater National Bank, I was in Biloxi, Mississippi, playing in a pro-am. My partners were the athletic directors of the University of Mississippi and Mississippi State University. A conversation came up about players getting money and "cush" summer jobs from boosters.

I hadn't told a soul about getting that sweet deal on the Corvette at Oklahoma State for fear of getting someone in trouble. But I decided to tell my story, thinking I was one up on these guys. I went through the whole tale about meeting with Mr. Gass and getting the loan from Mr. Lucas.

When I finished, the men looked at each other and one of them said, "Danny, if you had been here, you might never have had to pay that money back!"

CHAPTER SEVEN

MY OPEN DEBUT, THEN TRAVEL SHOCK

Cameo Moments and Survival on the Road

✦ ✦ ✦ ✦ ✦

What I call "cameo" moments are when someone or something unexpectedly enters my world, leaving a phrase or impression that sticks to my ribs.

During the summer of 1971, the Trans-Mississippi Amateur Championship was played at the superb Brook Hollow Country Club in Dallas. Tournament Director Jimmy Vickers had invited Ben Hogan to come over from Fort Worth for the opening cookout the afternoon before the tournament.

Gary Koch, Ben Crenshaw, and I were sitting together when Mr. Vickers came over and asked if we wanted to meet Mr. Hogan. We jumped at the opportunity. I assumed that Ben had probably already met him, but Gary and I were awestruck.

We shook Mr. Hogan's hand and just stared at him. Finally, Mr. Vickers said, "Well boys, has the cat got your tongue? Don't you have a question for Mr. Hogan?"

I couldn't think of anything to ask. Finally, Gary said, "Mr. Hogan, how much did you practice back when you were our age?"

Hogan looked at each one of us straight in the eyes and said, "Well boys, only when it was light!" I shook Mr. Hogan's hand again and headed to the putting green.

Just four years after I began hitting balls with my neighborhood friend, Paul Walters, I was on my own fast lap in golf. The summer of 1973, the year I graduated from Oklahoma State, was my springboard to professional golf.

Dr. Rex Kenyon lived and practiced in Edmond and was an avid golfer, playing mostly at Kickingbird Golf Course. PGA Professional Art Proctor introduced us and shared some of my golf accomplishments.

Art explained that I was interested in playing the British Amateur, but entries had closed. And although the Open Championship entries were still open, I didn't have the money to travel to Scotland.

Dr. Kenyon asked, "What do you think it would cost to go over there and qualify?" I threw out a sum of $500, and you have to remember that this was 1973, and $500 was a chunk of change.

Dr. Kenyon looked at Art and then looked me right in the eyes and said, "Danny, I want you to go qualify!" It was another cameo moment.

In 1973, the wonderful links in South Ayrshire, Scotland, 32 miles southwest of Glasgow, hosted the last Open Championship under the name Troon Golf Club. Five years later it became the Royal Troon Golf Club.

There were four qualifying sites with around 125 players at each course for 24 spots each. Growing up in Oklahoma, I was comfortable in the Scottish wind. But the sand bunkers were shaped like nothing

I'd ever seen and were very penal. If a player got in one and was unlucky, he might end up having to play out sideways or even backwards.

My morning round of 71 at the Gailes Course, some five miles north of Troon, put me in about sixth or seventh place. Not bad. Another round in that neighborhood and I'd be in.

The Gailes Links Golf Course was a typical Scottish layout with with gorse and penal bunkers. The win was punishing that day. My strategy was to play conservatively, and considering the weather, par was a pretty good score. I went out in the second round with the same strategy and played well.

With three holes to go I was even par. The 16th was a long par-4 into the wind with three menacing pot bunkers diabolically positioned 20, 30 and 40 yards diagonally across the fairway, directly in front of the green.

What made the hole even more challenging were the little white out of bounds stakes about five steps directly behind the green in full view. My second shot to the 16th was a good one but the wind knocked it down and into the right bunker 40 yards from the green. It was not a deep bunker, but that straight face was more than intimidating. Fortunately, I was back in the bunker far enough that I could play a bit of a knockdown type of shot in hopes of keeping it under the wind, but the out-of-bounds stakes I had to clip it just right.

I did. It came out just as I saw it in my mind, skipped a couple times and went right in the cup for a birdie 3. Pars on the last two holes gave me a 70 for third low qualifier at my course. I was in the Open Championship at Troon Golf Club!

I slept like a rock that night and was up early for a practice round that morning at Troon.

On one of my practice rounds at the qualifying course I had run into Richard Harvey, the tournament director for the Porter Cup Invitational in Lewiston, New York. We always called him "Grandpa." Richard told me if I qualified I could stay where he was staying close to Troon.

So, I moved my things over after I'd qualified and met the nice people who ran the house. The next morning the wife fixed a great breakfast with fruit, juice, pastries, eggs, waffles, and bacon.

I headed off to the course, got registered and was shown to the locker room, where a small Scottish man with an accent I couldn't understand took me to my locker.

My assigned caddie and I headed to the driving range to warm up. In those days the caddies went out on the range and shagged the balls as we hit them. Each of the caddies had a bag and they either caught the balls on the fly in their bag or after a bounce or two. This practice was a little intimidating for me at first because I had never hit to a shagger with other caddies standing close by shagging for their player.

After I warmed up, we walked over to the putting green and hit some putts. Standing there on the putting green, looking back at the clubhouse and the gigantic grandstands around the 18th green, I thought about how golf began in Scotland centuries ago. It's the land where Bob Jones, Ben Hogan, Arnold Palmer, Gary Player, and Jack Nicklaus made their imprint by winning Open championships.

My pairing for the first two rounds of the 104th Open Championship included Bruce Devlin from Australia. I don't remember the third member of our group. The wind on this July morning was blowing and the temperature was in the 50's and low 60's. The course was fantastic with the famous "Postage Stamp" par-3 eighth hole and the railroad tracks along a couple holes on the back nine. It was unusual in that there were so many blind shots and really nothing much to aim at but a bush on a hill or landmarks in the distance. I shot 75 in both the first and second rounds and made the first cut.

The highlight of the first round was when 71-year-old Gene Sarazen made a hole-in-one at the Postage Stamp. A roar echoed around the course.

In those days there was a second cut after the third round to around 50 players, and ties for the final round, which in those days was on Saturday. My 71 in the third round on Friday was good enough to make the second cut and made me the only amateur to make the final round.

> **I was paired again with Bruce Devlin for the final round. My second shot to the first green was nice and I got a surprising reception as I walked onto the green. On the second hole my shot to the green was nothing spectacular, but the reception again was unexpected. I must have had a puzzled look on my face because Bruce said, "They're clapping for you. They are great, knowledgeable fans over here, and everyone knows you are the Low Amateur. The gallery will probably clap like that for you on every green today."**
>
> **He was right.**

I shot 75 again and finished tied for 39th in the championship. After I hit my second shot to the 18th, which came to rest about 100 yards from the green, the entire grandstand gave me a standing ovation! I'll never forget it.

At the presentation ceremony, I sat by the 18th green with runners-up Johnny Miller and Neil Coles and winner Tom Weiskopf. As I accepted the sterling silver medal as Low Amateur, I wondered if anyone back home had any idea what I was experiencing?

The following morning, I loaded my clubs and suitcase into a car for a ride to the airport. My hosts seemed a little nervous. Finally, the wife said, "Danny, did you understand the terms?"

I thought, what are the terms? Then it dawned on me that unlike all the homes I'd stayed in at the amateur tournaments over the past three years, these accommodations were not complimentary. How dumb could I be?

I apologized and asked how much I owed. We had a laugh and big hug, and I headed to the airport with $2 left in my pocket.

✦ ✦ ✦ ✦ ✦

AS SUMMER drew to a close, I was selected as one of 10 best amateur golfers in the country to represent the United States against Great Britain and Ireland in the Walker Cup. Because the United States Golf Association scheduled this event in August, opposite the PGA Tour qualifying school, the two or three members of the team who could have played both had to choose.

I've never regretted my decision to play in the Walker Cup, because I wanted to represent my country. It was well worth having to wait a year to try to qualify for the Tour.

The Country Club in Brookline, Massachusetts, was the site of the 24th edition of the Walker Cup. It was a beautiful golf course, and besides its rich history—native son Francis Ouimet won a landmark 1913 U.S. Open there—it would later captivate golf fans with the unforgettable 1999 Ryder Cup.

I was 22, and one of five collegiate players named to the team.

When "The Star Spangled Banner" was played during the opening ceremony, there wasn't a dry eye among us.

At the welcome dinner at Locke-Ober restaurant in Boston, Great Britain and Ireland's Willie Milne and Charlie Green sat directly across the table from me. I watched Green drink two tall glasses of what looked like iced tea without the ice. It turned out to be straight Scotch. He didn't miss a shot the next day.

Jimmy Ellis, a senior at Georgia Southern, was my playing partner in the opening morning foursomes against the two. "There's no way I'm going to tee off first on that first tee!" declared Ellis, ``I'd be shaking like a leaf in a windstorm!"

So, I took a deep breath and somehow my drive found the middle of the fairway.

This being an international match, both teams had the option of playing the small British ball or the larger American ball. We chose to play the smaller ball, but I don't remember why. Possibly it was because Jimmy was a long hitter and we thought it would give us an advantage.

Any advantage may have been slight, but in the alternate shot or foursome matches when I found myself hitting several of Jimmy's drives out of the rough, the small ball nestled down more in the grass and made those shots a bit tougher.

The match was a close one all the way, but we were able to pull out a 2 and 1 victory over Milne and Green and get our point for the team. Our team won three of four foursome matches and tied one, so we led 3½ to ½, for the morning.

Rodney Foster, a veteran Walker Cup player, was my opponent for the afternoon singles matches, and I knew I had to bring my best game. I had a good, tough match and ended up beating him 2 up. Another point for our team!

Only Vinny Giles, Dick Siderowf and I won our afternoon singles matches, so we slipped back to a one-point lead of 6½ to 5½ after the first day. We were tired puppies and there wasn't much celebrating that evening. But I was feeling good.

On the final morning Jimmy and I were excited to be playing together again. Our guys all played well in the foursomes matches, and we came away with 3 ½ points, including the point Jimmy and I earned with our 2 and 1 victory over Peter Hedges and Michael King. Going into the final afternoon of the 1973 Walker Cup, the Americans were leading 10-6.

I drew reigning British Amateur Champion Trevor Homer in my fourth and final match of the event. Homer was a big fellow and a very strong player. We had a good match, back and forth, but I prevailed for another 2 and 1 victory to complete a winning sweep of all four matches, two foursomes and two singles. I was the only player to win all four of my matches, and our team recorded a 14-10 victory.

The honor of representing my country in these patriotic competitions is one of my most cherished experiences in golf. Hardly a day goes by that I don't glance at that Walker Cup Team picture and the sterling silver cup in my office.

Forty-eight years later, the Walker Cup came to Seminole Golf Club in Juno Beach, Florida. It was a wonderful reunion of the members of our 1973 team: Dick Siderowf, Martin R. West III, Vinny Giles, and Gary Koch.

Barely catching a breath, I was back on the course a week after the Walker Cup in the U.S. Amateur at Inverness Club in Toledo,

Ohio. The field played 36 holes of medal play and the 64 lowest scores advanced to match play.

I qualified and then won my first couple of matches. My third match was with a local fellow who made his living as a plumber. We both played very well, and he holed two shots from the fairway, a 9-iron and a 6- or 7-iron, both for eagles. I think I was 5-under par for the day and got beat. That's what can happen in match play.

That tournament marked the conclusion of an amateur career that I could have only dreamed of four years before. A scholarship to play golf at Oklahoma State University set so many rewards and opportunities in motion: being a three-time All-American; competing in three U.S. Amateurs and the 1972 U.S. Open; finishing Low Amateur in the Open Championship; winning two major amateur titles – the 1972 North and South and the '72 Southeastern Amateur – and being first alternate on the 1972 World Amateur Team and a member of the 1973 Walker Cup Team.

As an interesting sidebar, many amateur colleagues and several golf magazine writers contacted me in the succeeding days, after I was passed over by the USGA for an outright spot on the '72 World Amateur Team.

The four players were announced the day after the finish of the '72 U.S. Amateur Championship at Charlotte Country Club: Vinny Giles, Ben Crenshaw, Mark Hayes, and Martin R. West, III, whose father happened to be on the USGA executive committee. West hadn't won anything of note other than a couple of Maryland State Amateurs.

Only Ben Crenshaw, and possibly Vinny Giles, with his U.S. Amateur win at Charlotte, had a better record in '71 and '72 than me. My two major amateur tournament victories and several top-5 amateur finishes in the country's premier events lifted me miles ahead of Mr. West.

I had finished 11th in the U.S. Amateur at Charlotte, and all the guys, including Golf World writer Dick Taylor, had congratulated me afterward for being a lock onto the World Amateur Team. No one could believe I had been passed by.

After a week or so, I decided to write USGA Executive Director P.J. Boatwright a letter to express my disappointment. His return letter was one that I'll never forget:

"Dear Danny,
You can be assured we are as objective as we can possibly be."
P. J. Boatwright Jr.

✦ ✦ ✦ ✦ ✦

AS I MENTIONED EARLIER, my decision to play on the 1973 U.S. Walker Cup Team resulted in my having a year to kill before the 1974 Q-School.

I devoted the rest of my time to playing mini-tours, joining a couple buddies to test our games first in Del Mar, California, and ultimately on the Asian Golf Tour, a 10-week commitment that included the Philippines, Hong Kong, Singapore, Indonesia, Malaysia, India and more.

My friends John Lynch and Don "The Colonel" Klenk—nicknamed after Colonel Klink of *Hogan's Heroes*—met me in San Francisco. From there we headed to Manila. Little did we know what was in store for us halfway around the world.

Upon our arrival in Manila, we learned that President Marcos had imposed martial law on the city. We made it to the course, Wack Wack

Golf and Country Club, and met tour director Skip Ginto at registration. After we picked up our credentials, Skip motioned us to a corner.

"I want you boys to be careful," he said quietly. "A King cobra snake bit one of the caddies the other day and he died near the seventh hole. So just be careful!"

John was white as a ghost. Don looked at me like he had just made the biggest mistake of his life.

After surviving that piece of news, the guys wanted to get out on the town. I wasn't very interested, with the martial law and everything else going on, but I didn't want to be stuck in the hotel alone.

Five of us piled into a taxi and headed for a "gentleman's club." I wondered what I was getting into. After 20 minutes of dodging cars and motorbikes, the driver turned abruptly to the right into a narrow alley. The doors could barely open enough on each side to let us squeeze out.

After the taxi shot off, we were left looking at a wide row of white steps leading up to two glass doors. Inside was a nicely decorated greeting room with at least a dozen lovely young ladies. To our astonishment, they started conversing with us in English. One asked me where I was from. "America." Oh, what state in America? "Oklahoma." Are you a golfer? "Yes." Blah, blah, blah!

When I said I played at Oklahoma State she lit up. "Do you know J.R. Shade?" Halfway around the world this girl knew that poker-playing fellow on my college golf team who never went to class his final semester!

I don't remember much about how I played in Manila. I know we had no tournament wins. The uncertain atmosphere sapped me of the concentration I had been accustomed to bringing to the game. Mostly we just tried not to have something weird happen to us.

Hong Kong was interesting and very congested. Our hotel was downtown and it was about a 30-minute non-stop train ride to Hong Kong Golf Club. Each morning we passed little floating shacks, the homes of the "boat people." By the time we got out to the course we were feeling like pretty privileged guys.

The course was lovely, with big eucalyptus trees lining the fairways. From the driving range we could see the red flag of Communist China waving atop a hill in the distance.

I recall that John Lynch got mad at his caddie one time, and the caddie dropped John's big red and white Wilson tour bag and walked off, leaving John to carry the bag the last four holes. Don and I got a real hoot out of seeing our buddy carrying his bag up the 18th fairway.

Singapore was a beautiful city, and our hotel was nice. Unfortunately, John got dehydrated in the sweltering heat and ended up in the hospital. His parents told him in no uncertain terms to return home. We wished him Godspeed as he got into the taxi to the airport.

The golf course in Singapore must have been near an open zoo or game preserve because we saw a hippopotamus standing not 30 yards behind the first green in some type of lagoon. We had also heard that a black panther had been shot and killed on the course the week before we arrived.

I don't remember much about the golf tournaments themselves considering all the distractions.

The next week in Medan, Indonesia, one of the buses taking players to the course hit a boy and girl riding a motor scooter and killed them, or so we were told. The witnesses on the bus said it didn't even stop. It was starting to seem as if playing a golf tournament in this part of the world wasn't that important, considering what the people dealt with every day.

(continued on page 125)

Before I devoted my athletic career to golf, I was committed to basketball.
I cherish many Edmond High School memories on the court.

Edwards Bags Individual Title By Six Strokes

By Wallis Wallis
Staff Writer

STILLWATER — Danny Edwards of Edmond shot a two-under-par 68 to win the Class A high school golf championship by six shots at Lakeside Memorial course Tuesday as the Stillwater Pioneers swept the team competition.

Edwards, a slender and stylish swinging senior, trailed the leader by four shots with his 75 in the first round and by two strokes after the second round Monday during which he shot a 76.

His 68, only sub-par round to be played in the 1969 tournament, gave him a nine-over-par 219 on the 6,600 yard course which demands a par of 35-35—70.

Stillwater's well-balanced foursome of Henry Delozier, Craig Struthers, Danny Tewell and Phil Delozier raced to the four-man title with ease as Henry Delozier shot 225, Struthers 233, Tewell 234 and Phil Delozier 238 to give the Pioneers a 54-hole total of 930 and a 12-shot edge over second place Ada (942).

My senior year, 1969, included a state golf championship and joining Hayden Abney as Mr. and Mrs. Edmond High School.

Edmond High School

Edmond, Oklahoma

RAYMOND McKEE
COUNSELOR

Mr. E H S for 1969 is

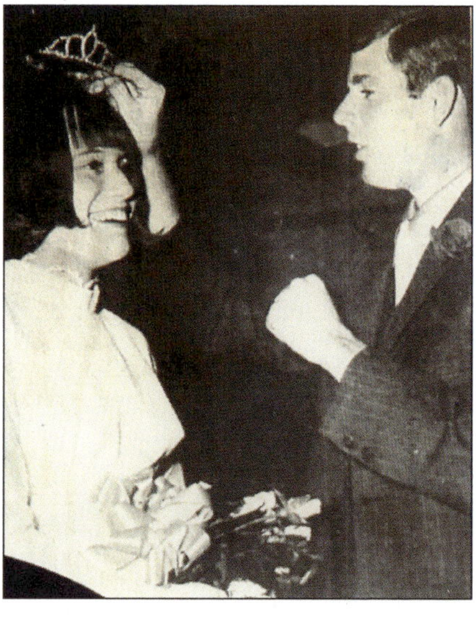

The first time I was on the cover of a national golf magazine.
Three years out of high school, and I was enjoying one of the great golf weeks of my life by winning the 1972 North & South Amateur Championship in Pinehurst.

GOLF WORLD (2)

A Golf World photographer captured my attention on my way to winning the 1972 North & South Amateur Championship, while legendary golf writer Dick Taylor not only covered the event but also hosted me that week in his home.

Getting up and down around the Donald Ross-designed greens is vital for any chance of success on Pinehurst No. 2. I was fortunate to do it often enough in my week at the 1972 North & South Amateur Championship.

THE COUNTRY CLUB (BROOKLINE) ARCHIVE

One of the great weeks of my golfing career, representing my country in the 1973 Walker Cup at The Country Club in Brookline, Massachusetts. Front row, left to right: Mike Killian, Vinny Giles, Dick Siderowf, Marty West III. Back row, left to right: Gary Koch, myself, Mark Pfeil, Bill Rogers, Jimmy Ellis, Doug Ballenger, Captain Jess Sweetser

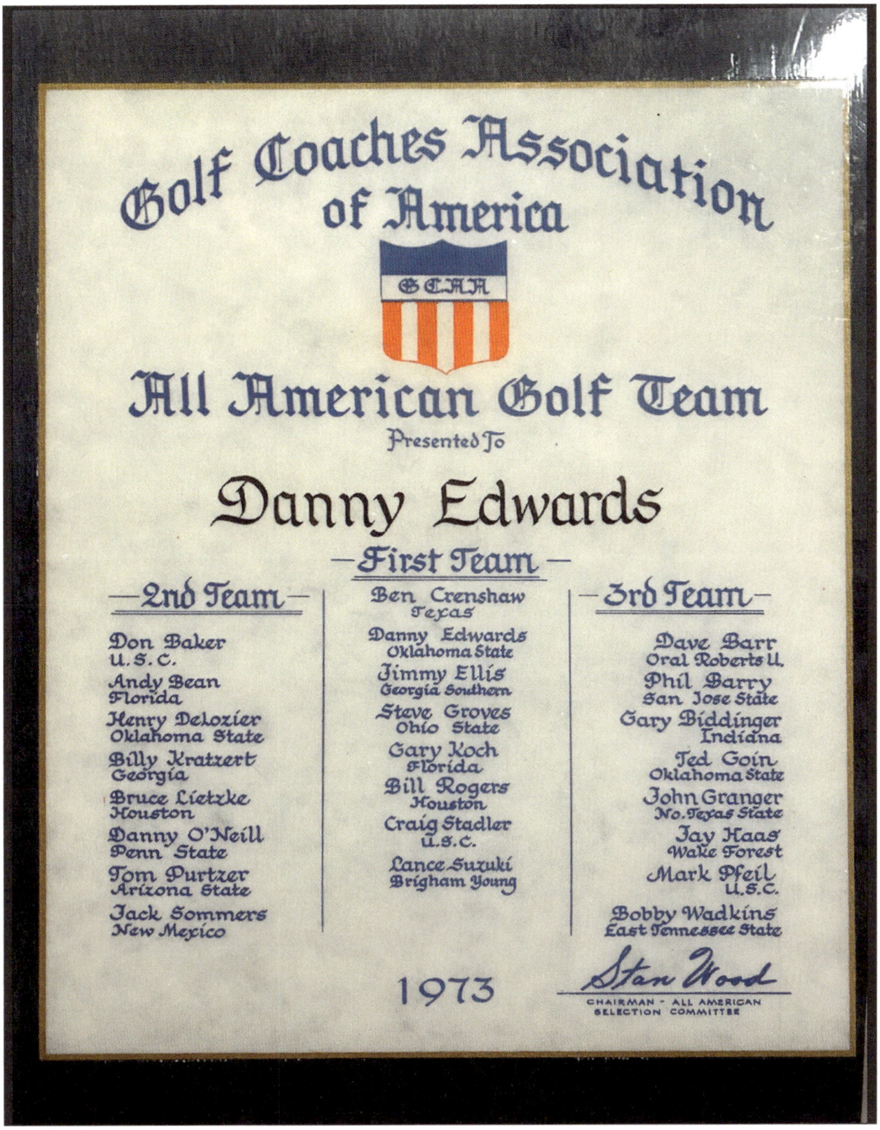

The culmination of hard work and great memories during my senior year at Oklahoma State. Earned a first-team berth on the Golf Coaches Association All American Golf Team, and was proud that teammates Henry DeLozier (second team) and Ted Goin (third team) were also recognized.

GETTY IMAGES

For some reason, I felt comfortable making my debut in the Open Championship in 1973 at Troon Golf Club in Scotland. Finished the week at the Low Amateur (tied for 39th) on my first trip overseas. This was the course's last Open Championship under the name Troon Golf Club; it became Royal Troon Golf Club five years later.

My medal moment at the 1973 Open Championship, finishing Low Amateur and tied for 39th at Troon Golf Club.

The 1974 Open Championship at Royal Lytham & St. Annes, my second consecutive trip to golf's oldest major. I was paired in the final round with Taiwan's Liang-Huan Lu, "Mr. Lu," a crowd favorite. Our games couldn't have been more different, but we each shot 73 and shared fifth place.

GETTY IMAGES (2)

Chatting with the gregarious Hubert Green on the practice range at the 1974 Open Championship. That's quite the cap for Hubie, who was such a tremendous player. In the background, that's Jack Nicklaus warming up.

Unbeknownst to me, this original Janet Bond DeWitt painting, which now hangs in my home office, graced the walls of the foyer for years at Golf World headquarters in Southern Pines, North Carolina.

Car No. 38 was my first new Formula Ford race car. I was excited to have Oklahoma Land Exploration Company as my sponsor for my second season in running the SCCA Formula Ford regional and national series.

One of the few times you'll find an image like this — me in a racing suit and carrying a helmet, while alongside three racing legends in street clothes — (from left) Danny Sullivan, Rick Mears and to my left, Bobby Rahal. These amazing athletes own a combined seven Indianapolis 500 titles (Bobby also got one as an owner). They supported our Michigan 500 Pro-Celebrity Golf Classic by coaching us in the Drivers School at the Michigan International Speedway.

GOLF WORLD

I have many fond memories of Greensboro, North Carolina, and it began by winning the first of two Greater Grensboro Opens in 1977.

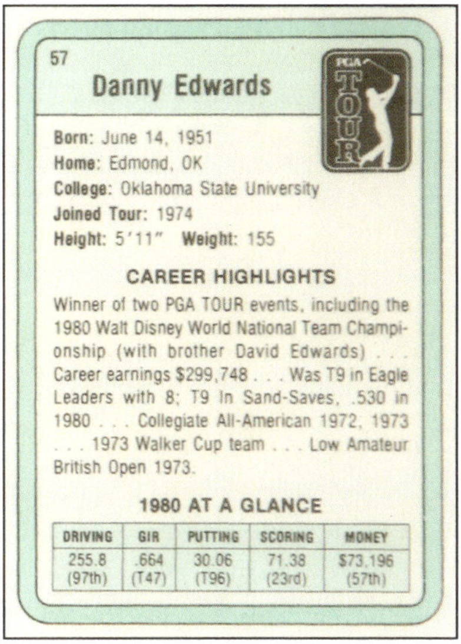

The top 60 money winners on the PGA Tour in 1980 were featured in a trading card collection. I was one of the 60 and had every player sign his card for me.

A great day, celebrating with my brother David after winning the 1980 Walt Disney World National Team Championship. Joining us were Card Walker, chairman of Disney (far left), me, Mickey Mouse, David and David's wife, Jonnie.

Pebble Beach is one of the special golf destinations in the world, and I was fortunate to play there often with Roger Penske (far right) as my partner in the Bing Crosby National Pro-Am. During one year, our foursome featured 1986 Indy 500 Champion Bobby Rahal (far left) and PGA Tour Professional Bob Eastwood.

Golfers mixed with drivers and tennis star Andy Mill (behind me with sunglasses) at the Michigan 500 Pro-Celebrity Golf Classic. The golfers were thrilled beyond belief when they received their own personalized racing suits and helmets. We delivered one of the best charitable events of its kind and benefited Foote Memorial Hospital in Jackson, Michigan. Some of the notables joining me: Rick Mears (far left), Rocco Mediate, Bill Rogers, Bruce Lietzke, Bob Tway, Harry Taylor, Bobby Rahal, Bob Gilder, Mike Hulbert, Mark Hayes and Jerry Haas.

Hanging with "RP" in the pits at a 2016 IndyCar race in St. Petersburg, Florida.

With Chris Kaufmann, one of my longtime friends and who has caddied for me in numerous professional golf tournaments. Chris helped me better understand racing strategy and technique, and allowed me to team with him during many of the most fun years I had on the track.

Three months after winning the 1982 Greater Greensboro Open, I am making final preparations before the start of the 1982 June Sprints at Road America in Elkhart Lake, Wisconsin. This was the largest amateur auto race in the United States. I led every lap and won the race against 124 competitors.

During my 41st birthday, I was honored to have Karsten Solheim as a guest that day. We developed a nice relationship by virtue of my being one of the early PGA Tour professionals to play PING golf clubs.

Above: We spread the message as strongly as possible about Royal Grip. Our proprietary compound and innovative manufacturing processes made an impact in the golf industry and drove our meteoric ascent.

Left: PING gave me a wonderful congratulatory ad following my win in the 1985 Pensacola Open.

My first Executive Golf Outing was conducted at the La Quinta Resort in Palm Desert, California. It was attended by 16 Ford dealers who had won a contest at our event and included Ford CEO Harold A. Poling.

My mom, Donna Mae McCandless Edwards, my inspiration and unconditional supporter, at DC Ranch in Scottsdale, Arizona.

The moments a teacher finds fulfilling — giving a tip to junior golfers and seeing them find fun and grow in the process.

With brother David, proud to share a combined 16 professional wins and 75 years on the PGA Tour and PGA Tour Champions

With Mery, my love, spending time together with my lifetime game and her newfound sport.

(continued from page 108)

Ipoh, Malaysia was my last tournament. I was feeling awful as I left the airport and got on a bus for an hour-long ride to the course. There was no air conditioning, and the rough road did no favors for my already-queasy stomach.

We had been told that we would be staying at the course, so we were imagining a nice resort with accommodations like those at home. When we arrived, there was no one in sight. The bus drove around to the side of a one-story, flat-roofed building, where we saw a card table with a light bulb dangling above it from a wire. Keys were lying in a pile on the table.

My roommate, Randy Geiselman, grabbed a key. As we went toward the covered walkway separating two sad-looking structures, we noticed that the walls looked unusual. When we got closer, we realized that they were covered with mosquitoes.

Once we found our room we darted inside and closed the door. Fortunately, there was a window air conditioner, and the mosquitoes stayed mostly on the ceiling.

Most of my first night was spent on my knees in the tiny bathroom puking my guts out. The next day, Monday, I didn't leave the room. Tuesday was not much better, so I hired a ride into town to see a doctor. At the office I sat in the heat for 30 minutes before someone showed me to a little area in the back, where the doctor checked my vitals and gave me the once-over.

"You are sick, and you need to go home," he said. That was all I needed to hear. That afternoon I was on a plane to San Francisco.

The experience of spending time in other countries has given me appreciation for the beauty, safety, conveniences, organization, and respect for laws that we take for granted in our country.

✦ ✦ ✦ ✦ ✦

FOLLOWING MY Low Amateur finish in the Open Championship the summer before, I was eager to see what I could do in the '74 Open at Royal Lytham and St. Annes. There were four more tournaments after the Open Championship—the Swiss, German, Scandinavian and Dutch Opens—that I could play if I qualified. I decided those five tournaments would make for a good trip.

My friend Mark Rolfing and I had met up in England and planned to room together for the five tournaments. Mark came back to the room one evening and said excitedly, "Danny I've got the backswing figured out! Watch this!"

I was lying in bed watching TV. There was only one light in the room, a bulb hanging down from the ceiling on a cord. When Mark took his backswing the club hit the light, shattering it into a million pieces. The room went pitch black immediately and the glass rained down on me.

That episode was the perfect preamble to playing in an Open Championship at Royal Lytham and St. Annes in cold and rainy weather the entire week.

Gary Player played the final two holes of survival to win the Claret Jug, beginning with apparently losing his second shot left of the difficult 17th green. He got a reprieve when his caddie, Rabbit Dyer, located the ball. He nearly lost the championship again on the 18th hole when his approach shot on the par-4 rolled over the green onto a gravel walkway, which was out of bounds. But after hitting the corner of the clubhouse, the ball caromed back in bounds.

I had finished two groups ahead of Gary and was standing under the scaffolding not 10 feet from his ball. I couldn't believe it when I saw it rolling toward the clubhouse.

Gary was the only player under par for the Open. I had played well in my second Open Championship and finished fifth in a major. With Low Amateur in '73 and fifth place in '74, I was ready for Switzerland!

One early evening at dusk in Crans, Switzerland, as I prepared for the Swiss Open, I was walking back through the quaint mountain town to my little hotel, when I was stopped dead by the sound of a screaming V12 Ferrari Daytona fast approaching through the narrow street. It was the most beautiful sound that could come from an automobile, and it was a sign for what would come in my life. Count it as another of my cameo moments.

The Swiss Open proved to be a bountiful trip. I received a check for $2,500 for finishing fifth and another one for $1,500 for a hole-in-one I made during the final round. I boarded a train that evening to Krefeld, Germany, for the German Open. Upon arrival I headed to my hotel, where Mark Rolfing was waiting.

The next morning, I couldn't find my two checks. I searched everywhere. So, I eventually reached the tournament office in Crans, explained the situation, and was told that they would be replaced. However, there would be a six-month delay until I got the money.

Back home, when I finally received the funds, I saw that $4,500 had been wired into my account. I had made an extra $500 because the Swiss franc had appreciated delightfully.

Three Penn Life Insurance agents sponsored me in my first year —Paul Creasy, Jim Eckenrode, and Bill Gustafson. Bill made the trip to the Dutch Open in Hilversum, Holland, to support me at the conclusion of my five-tournament swing in Europe.

Bill was a good friend who had put together my sponsor team over a three-year period. They were great guys, and after my first season of earning $27,000 on the PGA Tour and another $53,000 in pro-ams and other events, I bought out my contract.

The members of my team each put in $2,000 originally, and because I started earning money right away they didn't have to put anything more in the pot. After that first season, I exercised my option to buy out of the contract, repaying them $5,000 to cover my debts.

CHAPTER EIGHT

MY NEED FOR SPEED AND GETTING TO KNOW THE CHIEF

Escaping Hazards on the Open Road

✦ ✦ ✦ ✦ ✦

Kickingbird Golf Course opened in 1971 in Edmond, Oklahoma, two years after I graduated from high school. My brother, David, worked at the course and got help with his game from PGA Professional Art Proctor.

One day, Art introduced me to Jerry Matheson, chief of the Oklahoma Highway Patrol. Jerry was an avid golfer and a very good player. We became good friends and Art would join us often for nine holes.

I had graduated from Oklahoma State and been out on the Tour a year or two when I got a call from Jerry one day. "Can you play next week? I have a game set up."

I accepted without hesitation. Jerry suggested I bring an old carry bag and shoes. Hmm, something was up. Jerry explained that a couple big-time lawyers from Ardmore wanted to play, and he needed some help.

We met up at Oak Tree Golf Club, on the north side of Edmond, and had a chance to talk before the big shots showed up. He said these guys were good players who thought they were great, and that he would take care of the bets.

The lawyers arrived in a big yellow Lincoln Town Car. We could tell they were pretty confident.

After the introductions, away we went. Both teams parred the first few holes. As one of the lawyers walked up the third fairway with me he asked, "Didn't you play at Oklahoma State?"

"Yes, sir, I did." He didn't say much more, just walked on.

After I birdied two of the last four holes on the front, I think we won a few bets. I didn't do much gambling at all. My focus was always on shooting the best score I could every time I went out to play. But I had an idea how the games went with the presses.

I got going on the back by making birdies on the 10th and 12th after presses and then on 14 and 16. The boys from Ardmore hadn't won a single hole and were not happy.

After we all teed off on the 18th, Jerry rode by in the cart and said, "Whatever you do on this hole, as soon as you hole out, I want you to head straight for your car and get out of here. I'll take care of things."

I played a nice 7-iron to 10 feet from the hole which would give me 30 on the back nine. Everyone else putted and I holed the 10-footer, walked over and picked up my bag, and headed for the parking lot.

I didn't see Jerry again until he showed up at Kickingbird the next week.

"How did we do?" He had the biggest smile I'd ever seen on his face.

Later, he presented me with one of his pins from the Oklahoma Highway Patrol. The pin had "No. 3 on it. He let me know that the governor was No. 1, the lieutenant governor was No. 2, and Jerry was No. 3.

I carried that pin for years in my wallet so, whenever I got stopped for speeding, the officer would see it. I admit, it got me out of some binds. It showed officers that I knew someone high up in the force, and that opened a line of communication. Officers knew Captain Matheson wouldn't have given a pin to a bad guy.

Once, I was stopped while driving my Ferrari out of Ponca City, Oklahoma, after a tournament. Two officers approached.

When I opened up my wallet, I could tell the officers noticed the pin immediately. One said, "Where did you get that?"

"Captain Matheson gave it to me. We're golf buddies."

They got a laugh out of that, and one patrolman said, "We thought you were an officer on the take driving a car like this."

✦ ✦ ✦ ✦ ✦

I'VE MADE THE 50-MINUTE DRIVE on I-35 from Edmond to Stillwater, Oklahoma, hundreds of times through the years. On one occasion I'd been on tour for several weeks and was excited to be home and behind the wheel of my jet-black Ferrari Testarossa.

There was something going on in Stillwater that I wanted to check out, so I left early in the morning. With light traffic and clear skies, it was a perfect time to let the beast breathe.

As the needle passed 100 mph, I noticed across the very wide median a highway patrol car heading southbound. Then a glance in the rearview mirror showed him making a hard left into the median to turn around and give chase.

I had to make a quick decision. Pull over and face the consequences, or put the pedal to the metal. Away I went toward the exit to Stillwater about four miles ahead.

Exit ramps are usually pretty flat anyway, and this long, fairly wide right-hand sweeper had been designed with enough banking to make possible a high-speed exit—although maybe not at 100 mph.

After I navigated the exit, the pedal went down again. Highway 51 was a divided four-lane for the remaining 12 miles into town. At the edge of town were a few motels, restaurants, and gas stations where I could hide the black beauty.

I pulled into a Holiday Inn Express and parked in the back. My heart felt like it was beating faster than the Ferrari.

The vacant lobby had a good view of the highway. After sitting there 15 minutes with a magazine in front of my face like some gangster in the movies, I walked out and looked around, then went around back, got in the car, and drove into town.

I would never suggest that anyone try a stunt like that. But what a rush!

My quest for speed began when I was a kid, ignited by being challenged in a footrace. It blossomed into racing my Schwinn Stingray bicycle, studying muscle cars, and purchasing my first car at 20, that British racing dark green 1971 Corvette LT1 350. Ultimately, I found myself navigating a four-mile course in a Formula Ford.

What was I doing racing and risking my hide at every turn while also playing on the PGA Tour?

I did it for the love and excitement of it. I loved trying to make that car go faster on the track than everybody else. I loved the sound of it and the feel of it and the challenge of keeping it on the course lap after lap.

It was a joy and a test to see if I could handle it for an extended period of time. Races can last from 30 to 45 minutes to several hours.

About halfway through the race you're passing the back markers and facing a whole new situation. You have to pick your openings and make decisions. You have to be focused and ready to react in a split second.

It's exhilarating to approach a turn flat-out as your eyes instantaneously communicate with your brain: "Slow down! You can't make it through this turn at this speed!"

You're not focused on what dangers may lie ahead. You're keeping the pedal glued to the floor as the car slides through the turn grabbing for traction.

You're gaining on the car ahead of you, and then you're making the pass and tearing off to set up and overtake the next challenger.

In golf, you have time to think about what to do. In racing, you have to train your reflexes. There's no time for analysis in a 1,129-pound machine as you power your way around the course. You have a fraction of a second to make a decision. You're running on adrenaline and instinct.

And if you make a mistake in a race car, you can pay the ultimate price, and many have. Every driver thinks about the danger each time they get into that cockpit.

My passion unequivocally was for golf. Racing was just a physical rush. It was a macho thing.

✦ ✦ ✦ ✦ ✦

JIM MCFARLAND, my uncle, was vice president and director of research and development for Edelbrock Corporation, a developer of high-end racing components in Southern California. He introduced me to Chris

Kaufmann, a former member of the Los Angeles Police Department and a professional racer.

Chris attended Arizona State University on a wrestling scholarship but had a passion for golf. He had a short stint as a PGA Professional in Southern California while building his high performance racing operation.

Chris and I met at a golf course in the 1980s and hit it off. He acted as an occasional Tour caddie/confidante/sports psychologist for me.

Our first time together on a track was at Willow Springs Raceway north of Los Angeles, a frequent test site for Kaufmann Racing. Chris invited me to come run a few hot laps in one of his Mustang race cars.

The Mustang, which was nearly three times the weight of my Formula Ford, was a struggle to handle at first. It was not built to be a purpose-driven race car, and it had a normal vehicle ride height, which made the handling more of a challenge.

"I never understood Danny's passion or background until that day at Willow Springs," says Chris. "I had multiple cars and testing components. I suggested that he take a few laps, and I would lead him and then he would follow.

"It was only a few minutes into our running that I found myself doing everything I could to follow a guy I had led around the track. I thought, 'Well man, this guy can race!"

We later put together a three-person team. One of the professional series we raced in was the Escort Radar Endurance Championship, which involved three, six, 12, and 24-hour races at some of the iconic tracks across the United States and Canada. Each of the

> **"Danny would have made a living as a professional race car driver had he elected not to play golf. He is a natural athlete and has incredible hand-eye coordination. Something that helped him for a long time is that he was able to memorize racetracks. He was one of the greatest students you could ever run across. He soaked everything up like a sponge."**
>
> ***—CHRIS KAUFMANN, PROFESSIONAL RACE CAR DRIVER, FORMER LAPD MEMBER***

three drivers on our team would race three hours in a car and then switch out.

We raced at Sears Point, Road Atlanta, Mid-Ohio, Riverside International Raceway, Pocono Raceway, Chicagoland Raceway, Mosport International Raceway in Canada, Road America, Laguna Seca, and many more.

We raced against big-bucks factory Corvettes, Camaros, Datsun Zs, and Porsches, and we managed to stay right there with them or ahead of them in competition.

Chris encouraged me to get a professional license, and pulled some strings to get me into the Bob Bondurant School of High Performance Driving in Phoenix, which used Roush Mustangs as school cars. The cars were the creation of Jack Roush, who began his racing career in 1964 as an engineer at Ford Motor Company.

Chris was good friends with head driving instructor Bill Cooper and had hired him to co-drive one of his Mustangs in the Escort series.

Bill and I developed good camaraderie and our skills meshed. The fellow drivers accepted that I could be competitive in the car. Soon, there were auto parts coming into our team to enable us to be competitive with other high-profile teams.

The stars were aligning. I had my racing license in order. I also had 300 or 400 test miles, and 40 or 50 pit stops in practice, including the tricky driver changes.

So, Chris decided to team Bill Cooper and me at the first race at Sears Point in Sonoma County, California, where Bill had home track advantage. It was the only West Coast track where I had practice time.

It was a perfect match. We started out near the back of the pack in 16th place and finished second out of 63.

Chris brought the team and cars to Atlanta for a big Escort Endurance Championship race. I had driven a few races with the team by then, and since I had raced at Road Atlanta previously I was excited to be back there.

At one of the pre-race conferences I sat next to Paul Newman, who was racing with his own team in a Datsun Z. There were about four of us on the dais, and all the questions from the media were directed at Newman. He was a very funny dude and as cool as he appeared in movies. I soon learned that he also was an excellent driver.

The practice sessions went well and I got a good feel for the car. This was a six-hour race, so there would be two drivers in each car, alternating two hours running and two hours off and possibly splitting the last two hours.

In the fifth hour of the race I was running very comfortably after my two-hour rest. I had lapped every other car except our sister team car and a Datsun Z, which I had caught. Our team car was in front of me as we came out of the right-hand turn going into the back straightaway, and the Datsun Z car was ahead of him.

As I accelerated through the gears to pass the Z-car on the left, our team car attempted to pass it on the right. I was almost past when the Z suddenly slammed into me, knocking me off the track at 130-plus miles per hour. The driver had been surprised when our team car pulled up on his right, and he instinctively jerked the wheel to the left and hit me.

I sailed out of control into the grass, almost flipping over and finally coming to rest with dirt and dust everywhere. The car was destroyed.

It had been a very dumb move on the part of our other team driver and cost us valuable points and thousands of dollars. Sadly, the Z-car also was taken out of the race. The other team driver never drove for us after that, and I don't recall ever seeing his name again, unlike so many we raced with who went on to have long careers.

Chris regretted that he never was able to get me a win, but we had numerous runner-up and podium finishes.

High-speed racing is part athletic and part-artistic. It's very intense, like the Tour, but in a much more physical way. When I was out playing a Tour event, the media would always ask me why I also pursued this dangerous hobby.

Part of the appeal was that racing and golf are both individual sports and that both require excellent hand-eye coordination, athleticism, and concentration.

Each year from 1979 to 1983, I played in 25 to 30 golf tournaments and drove in 10 to 12 races. Some said that I didn't devote enough time to my golf game, but playing as many as 30 golf events a year is a lot for anybody. It's just that I spent my off weeks on the racetrack.

Racing is simply a tremendous rush!

Chris and I had nicknames for each other. He called me "Enzo," after Enzo Ferrari, the legendary founder of Ferrari. Chris knew that I prized my Ferrari.

I bestowed a nickname on him after an episode when he was supposed to caddie for me.

I was playing a Tour event in Las Vegas, and Chris was flying to meet me that morning. At the airport in Los Angeles, he and six other passengers were ushered to a plane that was parked beside another with similar markings. There was no sign that indicated the plane's destination.

"We didn't know if we were on the right flight until the door closed," Chris later told me. "And once the door was closed, there was no getting off. It was 5:45 a.m., and our flight attendant announced that we were on a two-hour flight to Salt Lake City."

Chris said among the upset passenger group was a guy who had a huge business contract meeting and was trying to get the plane door open. He was looking like he would have a heart attack.

This was before cellphones were common, and Chris had no way to contact me until the plane landed in Salt Lake. By that time I had already left for the course. I ended up getting a guy who was standing by the clubhouse to caddie for me. When Chris finally turned up, I was well through my round.

It was then that I conferred upon him the nickname "Salt Lake."

✦ ✦ ✦ ✦ ✦

ONE MONDAY AFTERNOON I left California in the Ferrari Daytona, headed for the Dean Martin Tucson Open after my final round at the Andy Williams San Diego Open had been partially rained out that morning.

I got four speeding tickets that day.

The first was from a trooper who said, "I didn't quite clock you, but I know you have been speeding so I'm going to write you up anyway."

"You've got to be kidding," I said.

About an hour from Tucson, I noticed that a car was keeping pace far behind me. I was running around 110 to 120 mph. I figured I'd better slow down and see if it was a patrol car.

As the vehicle got closer, I could see two small blue flashing lights, so I shut down to 75 mph and waited for him to close up. When he came up behind me, I pulled onto the shoulder.

"What do you think you are doing?"

"Driving to Tucson, officer."

"One of our off-duty patrolmen passed you going north and estimated your speed at 130-plus!"

"So?" I said.

"Follow me. I'm taking you in to see the judge."

We slowly drove 10 miles into Eloy, Arizona. The courthouse was pretty much vacant as was the courtroom.

An elderly lady wearing a gray robe came in, sat down, and after writing something for a few minutes motioned for my new friend and me to approach the bench.

The officer explained the situation. The judge asked for my driver's license, which I handed to her.

"Oklahoma, what are you doing here in Arizona?

"Your Honor, I'm heading down to Tucson for a golf tournament."

"What kind of golf tournament?"

"The Dean Martin Tucson Open."

"Are you a professional?"

"Yes ma'am."

"Where do you live in Oklahoma?"

"In the Oklahoma City area, actually in a town called Edmond."

"Have you heard of a golf course named Oak Tree Golf Club?"

"Yes, ma'am. I live on the Oak Tree course."

"Do you know a man named Jack Freeman?"

"Yes, ma'am, Judge Freeman lives right down the street from me. We play golf often when I'm back home."

"He's my nephew," she said. I couldn't believe it.

"Mr. Edwards, just take it a little easier on our highways, will you please? And have a good tournament."

"Yes, ma' am. Thank you, judge." She handed me my license, and I turned around and left the courthouse.

I didn't wait to chat with my officer friend, but I remember the look in his eyes—pure shock.

CHAPTER NINE

IN THE KINGDOM OF ROYAL GRIP

Escaping Hazards on the Open Road

✦ ✦ ✦ ✦ ✦

After only 14 years playing full-time on the PGA Tour, never losing my exempt status, competing in 36 major championships, winning 20 worldwide professional tournaments—including five Tour events along with the Japanese Taiheiyo Masters—I decided to step away and start a company to make golf grips.

No one can imagine the frustration and heartbreak that drove me to make such a shocking decision. I had devoted my life to playing the game at a very high level and now I was giving up the competition that I loved.

I had fought a good fight, but I didn't feel that I had the complete game needed to accomplish what I had set out to do—win major championships. Maybe I retired too soon. Maybe I didn't.

My new mission was inspired by years of pursuing another passion, racing. In qualifying for those races, drivers need soft, "tacky" tires that grip the track. I got the idea for a soft grip in golf from different racing tire compounds.

The hard, slippery golf grips of the time tended to wear out quickly, and both production and quality were lacking. And while Tour professionals could change to new grips every other week for free if they desired at the repair trailers at tournament sites, the average golfer gets tagged to pay $50 to $100, or more, to change grips.

I was determined to develop a new material and process, with the goal of producing high-quality grips with better durability that would change the whole culture of what was expected from a golf grip.

I contacted an old friend, Dennis Livesey, a former engineer who had previous experience with grip manufacturing. We discussed the possibilities at length and decided to start a company, Royal Grip Inc., in the summer of 1988 in Scottsdale, Arizona. I funded the start-up with $50,000 and the contacts to introduce our product to the golf market.

It was a daunting task for two guys, one a retiree in his late 60s and the other a PGA Tour professional who had never had a real job.

We began by studying rubber compounding. Another critical piece of the puzzle was finding equipment that could produce the parts we needed.

In April 1990, after nearly two years of research and development, we felt ready to test our product with the players. I took two cases of grips to the Greater Greensboro Open and put them in one of the repair trailers. The range opened early Tuesday morning. Around 7:30 a.m. I spotted Sandy Lyle beginning to hit balls.

I grabbed my 7-iron, which had one of our grips on it, and walked over to greet Sandy. What do you think of this grip?" I asked.

"Feels really good," he said.

"I brought a supply, and I'll put some on your clubs if you want." I went back over to the trailer, and soon I saw Sandy coming over with his whole set.

"Put them on," he said.

I spent all day Tuesday and most of Wednesday changing grips for players. On Thursday morning, the Darrell Survey counted 32 players teeing off with at least one Royal Grip on their clubs and many with an entire set. Without a practice round that week, I finished tied for 47th in the championship.

We immediately started advertising in *Golfweek* and on radio. The orders started coming in. We hired East Coast, Central and West Coast sales representatives, then we brought on a handful of young men who had been assistant golf professionals at clubs and put them on the road calling on golf shops.

At the 1990 PGA Merchandise Show the president of Golf Pride announced that they would put Royal Grip out of business in six months. He would be eating those words in pretty short order as we picked up original equipment manufacturers (OEMs) and built strong relationships with hundreds of golf courses.

Later on, Golf Pride expressed interest in buying us. We had discussions, but it never got any further than that.

Royal Grip was progressing well with support from PGA Tour professionals, amateur golfers, and golf club manufacturers. It was time for us to spread our wings.

We had spent a year brainstorming in the two small offices in the airplane hangar I had rented at Scottsdale Airpark to house my collection of sports cars and muscle cars. Now we needed a building that would serve as an office and operations facility. We found suitable space nearby and contracted with a company in the San Francisco Bay Area to manufacture our grips to our specifications.

But there were problems. The company couldn't fill our shipping orders, and the quality was all over the map. The manufacturing technique that they employed required a time-consuming secondary process.

We had to organize dozens of workers to sit on folding chairs in a circle and use fingernail clippers to trim the flashings and clean every grip that showed up on our dock. I spent many hours in those chairs myself, and it was tedious work. We all ended up with blisters. But we were selling grips, lots of grips.

During this time, I would walk around the warehouse and see grips in boxes and on shelves everywhere. We would move dozens of big boxes of grips from the docks to the trimming area, to the weighing station, to the cleaning station, to the painting booth, to the packaging station, to the labeling area, and finally to the staging area for shipping. There would be thousands of grips on our warehouse floor at any time.

Although it was a great feeling to see all that product and remember the earlier days when we stood on the dock praying for a truck to pull in with a load of grips, I knew we were sadly inefficient.

In the spring of 1990, and to keep up with the growth we saw in the future, we realized we had to bring the manufacturing process in-house and avoid the poor quality and inconsistent delivery from our current supplier.

Our search for the vertical injection rubber molding machines that we needed to produce a finished product that did not require trimming led us to a distributor in Chicago for a company named REP. They made expensive, world-class rubber presses that stood about 15 feet tall and weighed 2,000 pounds apiece.

We also had to learn the process of making the cylindrical, seamless, nickel cavities with the shape, pattern, and texture of the grip, on the inside of the cylinder that would allow the finished grip to feel great right out of the mold. The molds also would have to be adaptable to carry our Royal Grip logo as well as other manufacturers' logos and graphics should we be able to attract them to our new product.

Identifying and solving problems was part of my job. I knew there must be a way to improve efficiency.

I discovered a system called cellular manufacturing and invited a company to give us a presentation. The system involved analyzing all the steps required to move a raw product through the manufacturing process to shipping.

The vendor studied the time it took to move a grip through our steps to a finished product. Then they set up a 15 x 15-foot cell and measured how long it took to have three people in the cell do all of the processes in that space. They reduced our start-to-finish manufacturing time from 50 hours to 15 minutes. The process was absolute magic.

As Royal Grip attracted more and more customers, we identified a much larger office and manufacturing space in Tempe, Arizona, that allowed us to move full speed ahead.

Over the next five years we found ourselve paying a workforce of more than 350 employees, speaking six languages, with the production of one million grips per month in our own plant. It was a great run, and the horizon looked bright.

We needed working capital, so I presented the business to three individuals who agreed to put $1 million in my account for a piece of the action. When my banker called to say the deposit had arrived, he said, "Do you know how unusual it is for someone to put $1 million into an account for a start-up business like yours?" No, I didn't.

We set up a competitive pricing strategy and didn't attempt to gouge our customers. We did $1.5 million in sales that first year, $6 million the second year, $9 million the third, and $12 and $15 million the next two years. Royal Grip made grips for 82 OEM manufacturers of golf clubs and built a very strong aftermarket business with thousands of golf courses and golf repair shops across the United States.

Almost every OEM today markets their clubs with grips that embody the feel and durability that Royal Grip pioneered 30 years ago.

✦ ✦ ✦ ✦ ✦

ENTREPRENEUR OF THE YEAR—1994

DURING 1993 AND 1994, Royal Grip Inc. got lots of publicity and recognition from magazines and newspapers. Reporters and TV stations wanted to interview us and come to the plant to photograph our operation. We exhibited at the PGA Merchandise Show each winter and also appeared at regional trade shows around the country. Pro shops adopted our product on a significant scale, and our market share grew toward 10 percent. We built strong relationships with manufacturers, golf courses, and players at all levels. And now Golf Pride and Lamkin were copying our product.

During this time, I played very little golf. For five or six years, I was wrapped up in building and promoting Royal Grip.

It was a fascinating operation for me as an untrained businessman, and I tried to continue to learn from Roger Penske and others I was fortunate to meet. Roger was not involved in any way with Royal Grip, but our friendship gave me a great opportunity to observe how he operated his business and dealt with his employees and staff.

While *Inc. Magazine* selected me the 1994 Entrepreneur of the Year for manufacturing in Arizona, any credit should be showered upon our outstanding and talented corporate and sales staff.

Bob Burg, who did a great job building the sales force, was my right-hand man. He and all the other young professionals were committed to Royal Grip and had a huge part in the success of the company, with their enthusiasm and ability to establish warm and loyal relationships with our customers and manufacturers.

✦ ✦ ✦ ✦ ✦

ROYAL GRIP MEETS PRECISION JAPAN

ONE DAY I GOT A CALL from a man with an Asian accent that wanted to purchase two million Royal Grips.

At $2 a grip, that was a substantial order, in those early days. I decided it would be wise to seek advice, so I called Dr. Joe Braley, founder of Precision Golf Shaft Company, who had become a good friend and confidante.

Dr. Joe said, "Don't do it, Danny." He explained how valuable our Royal Grip reputation could be overseas, especially in Japan, and that I need to be careful about who we chose to represent us.

On his advice, I turned down that $4 million order and often thanked Dr. Joe for his guidance.

Dr. Joe told me he knew the perfect person to be our distributor in Japan. He had set up Mr. Makoto Miyamoto—"Mako," as we called him — with the Precision shaft franchise in Japan, and Mako was interested in becoming the exclusive distributor for Royal Grips products in his country.

The first of my many trips to Japan went well, and we formed a partnership with Mako's company, Precision FM Japan, to represent Royal Grip Inc. Over the next few years, we built a strong relationship and did a terrific business supplying numerous OEMs and high-end golf repair stores with millions of our grips. Golf was exploding in Japan, and our timing was good.

Mako would set up meetings with his OEMs around the country, and the manufacturers would send me questions in advance about things they said they wanted to address, such as quality control and shipping schedules. I eventually learned that these questions were decoys. It was a bit sneaky, but part of the process. They wanted to make sure that Royal Grip was up to the task of providing the product they wanted in a timely manner.

We would meet in a conference room at the manufacturers' offices. Around the table would be a couple marketing guys, a couple engineers, and a couple corporate gentlemen. Around the perimeter of the room would be up to a dozen young men and women with their heads bowed over their notepads.

Mako also would arrange a press conference on every trip with 30 to 40 members of the media in the audience. An interpreter would translate my opening comments and then assist me with their questions.

The first year I decided to start with a funny story. I thought it was appropriate, and it had a good punchline.

The interpreter translated the story and I waited, expecting the reporters to laugh. They just sat there in their chairs, looking down.

I continued my remarks, and afterward I asked Mako if he understood my story, and thought it funny.

"Oh, yes that was a good story".

"Well, why didn't anyone laugh?"

"In Japan, it's not proper etiquette for pressmen to laugh at a press conference!"

Mako, his wife, Kyoko, and his brother, Mana, did a great job for Royal Grip in Japan, and our business grew to nearly the same volume as in the USA. Mako and Mana visited our facilities in Phoenix and I visited their operation at least twice every year.

Mako hosted a golf event every spring and fall for his customers, and I would attend. Playing golf over there is pretty much an all-day event, including a party afterward. The parties would include food, gifts for the customers, and plenty of toasts.

Each guest would rise and give a short speech to thank Mr. Miyamoto. The speeches were done in reverse order by seniority, and a toast was offered at the end of each. By the time everyone had said their peace, made their toast, and downed their sake, the room would be full of tipsy golfers. Except me. I kept my cup empty and faked drinking the toast each time.

✦ ✦ ✦ ✦ ✦

FROM A ROAD SHOW TO AN IPO

AFTER A GOOD BIT of discussion with our board in 1993–94, we decided to make shares of our stock available to the public.

Callaway Golf had had a successful initial public offering a few years earlier, as had Cobra Golf. The time seemed right, and all indications were that we had a good chance for a successful offering.

It was a heady two weeks for me, traveling the country and giving short presentations to brokers. The William Blair company of Chicago was our underwriter and set up the locations and brokers, from San Francisco to Boston and cities in between. We usually did at least two or three presentations a day.

The road show finished in Boston and that evening the lawyers, the guys from William Blair, and my advisor went to a pub to wind down. After nearly six years we were sitting on a company that might be worth $25 million or $30 million tomorrow!

The stock was oversubscribed, which was a good thing, and had been set to come out on the market at $13 a share. Speculation was that it might open a little higher because of the oversubscription. I owned one million shares, and we were selling one million shares to the public.

As it turned out, the stock ran to $22.50 the first day.

✦ ✦ ✦ ✦ ✦

FORSTMANN LITTLE

ONE AFTERNOON before our IPO, my secretary buzzed me and said there was a man on the line named Brian Little from Forstmann Little in New York. I knew that Vijay Singh played with a guy in the Crosby pro-am named Teddy Forstmann, and he was always mentioned along with his company, Forstmann Little. I figured Brian might be his partner.

Brian told me Forstmann Little was looking to buy the Aldila graphite shaft company and suggested that we might fit together well with them.

He came to Phoenix to see our operation, and as I showed him around I mentioned that we were seriously considering doing an IPO. We got the CEO of Forstmann Little on the phone and chatted for a while. We hit it off, so Brian suggested we move forward after our IPO and see if we could make something work.

Forstmann Little sent their people out to perform due diligence for a couple weeks and then said they were ready to make an offer. They wanted to present it at Aldila's headquarters in San Diego.

As we sat around the conference table, I was happy with the decision I'd made to merge Royal Grip with Aldila, sell my stake in the company, and get back to playing golf.

I had gotten a letter of intent putting the value of Royal Grip in the $14 million to $16 million range, and I was comfortable with those numbers. My share would be around $11,500,000 at the median price Forstmann Little had offered.

After some opening comments, the lead person laid an offer on the table for $8,900,000. There was dead silence.

At first I thought the offer was for just my share, but then I realized it was for the whole company. One of my advisors asked, "What happened to the signed letter of intent?" Nobody had an answer. The Forstmann Little spokesperson said, "That's what we are prepared to offer."

We adjourned to separate rooms, then decided to go back to Phoenix and consider the offer. We ended up turning it down.

During this time, we made contact with Belding Sports Golf Bag in Oxnard, California, a boutique custom equipment manufacturer that was for sale. I had our key manufacturing people visit Belding Sports numerous times, surveying their operation.

I also made several trips, visiting the Perrins, the owners of the company, learning their history, plans for the future, and finances.

We ultimately made an offer for the company, which they accepted. Several of us made the trip to Oxnard for a celebration of our new partnership. Early the next morning, I received a call from

Jack Perrin, to say that his 80-year-old wife had been crying all night with seller's remorse and she would die if we didn't cancel the deal.

After significant discussion, I decided to let them off the hook. Our deal was for something around $15 million, and two years later they sold the business for $35 million after our people found many ways that they could grow it and become more profitable.

One day I got a call from a man who introduced himself as Jim DeMelo, president of Acushnet Rubber Company. He explained they made all the cores for the Acushnet Golf Company, which manufactured golf balls.

He congratulated me on the success of Royal Grip and said he had been watching us for some time. He then invited me to come to New Bedford, Massachusetts, to see Acushnet Rubber Company's operation.

He explained that they were a 100-year-old company with contracts from all the major automotive companies, and that they believed they could make our golf grips for significantly less than they were currently costing us. He said the company had every manufacturing certification that existed, including the ISO 9000, along with a full rubber-compounding operation and full tooling capacity to make whatever we would need.

Because we were now a public company, I presented the opportunity to our board of directors to get their thoughts before pursuing the situation. Then, after visiting each other's facilities numerous times, we proposed that we send the company one of our 12 REP presses to see what they could do.

They were not interested in that proposal, saying that they needed all our equipment to make the effort worthwhile. However, I thought it was too big a risk to move our production of millions of grips to

Massachusetts, even though it seemed clear from their history, clients, and experience that the process should pose no problem for them.

My board agreed, and we politely passed.

Six months later, Mr. DeMelo reached out again with a sweetened offer. He said Acushnet Rubber Company had made arrangements to build out an area of their plant just for Royal Grip manufacturing, and that they had identified numerous improvements they could make that would benefit both companies.

After considerable study and discussion with our board, we decided to take the offer.

Mr. DeMelo had estimated that things could be up and running in four months from the time the presses arrived. We shut down our plant on December 20, 1995, loaded the 12 presses on six flatbed semi-trailer trucks, and sent them to New Bedford. We had built up eight months of inventory in case there were problems in Massachusetts.

At the time we were manufacturing around one million grips per month for our 82 OEM club manufacturers, aftermarket clients, and the operation in Japan, all sold out the door. It should have been a slam dunk for Acushnet Rubber Company.

But things started to go wrong within the first few months. For some reason they could not get the machines working properly. They had difficulty switching molds, and the quality of the parts was not acceptable.

The pressure grew as the weeks went by. We sent more than 30 people who had worked at our plant in Tempe to New Bedford for a few months, but the situation didn't improve much.

Over the next year, the highest number of quality grips they were able to produce per month was 500,000. It was half of what we needed and what we had been able to make at our plant. We lost every one of our OEM manufacturers because we could not guarantee delivery.

The stress and strain on everyone during the last half of 1996 was unbelievable. Acushnet Rubber Company paid us several million dollars in fines because they were not able to meet the terms of our agreement.

Our attorneys said, "If you sue Acushnet Rubber Company you will ultimately own them, because they have ruined your business. However, you will spend the next two years in courtrooms and in depositions."

During this disaster, which lingered through 1998, I got a call from Dick Johnston, who had purchased the Precision Shaft Company. He said they wanted to go public and asked if I would be interested in merging our two companies.

We met several times and decided to seal the deal. Some of our workforce stayed on with the blended company, whose new name was Royal Precision Inc.

I remained on the board for a couple years and then sold my shares for a fraction of what they would have been worth had our relationship with Acushnet been successful.

It had been a heartbreaking time for all of us. Not being able to realize the full measure of financial success we had built and share it with the many committed people who contributed to Royal Grip Inc. still haunts me.

But I licked my wounds and got back out on the golf course, three years away from eligibility for the senior circuit, what today is known as the PGA Tour Champions.

CHAPTER TEN

THE NEED FOR GREENFIX GOLF

Carving Another Niche in an Ever-Changing Industry

✦ ✦ ✦ ✦ ✦

During the manufacturing phase of my life, I got calls almost every week from people who had observed the company's success and were promoting some new and revolutionary product.

One of them was Terry Wiens, a professional who had played many years on the Canadian Tour and was a great friend of the legendary Moe Norman. Terry told some entertaining stories about his escapades with Moe, then got to the purpose of his call. He claimed that his product, the GreenFix Putter Grip, really was the greatest thing since sliced bread.

We agreed to meet in Palm Springs, where Terry demonstrated the tool. He was right; it was amazing!

Terry owned multiple patents on the tool and had tried to market it for several years without much success. He had followed my PGA Tour career and the success of Royal Grip Inc. and was confident that I was the guy to turn his product into a worldwide success.

The GreenFix Putter Grip had a hard plastic cap molded to the butt end of the grip, with a recessed area into which a small repair tool could be snapped. When a player wanted to fix a ball mark, he or she would snap the tool into place, turn the putter upside down, and push the edges of the mark back into the center of the depression.

Because the tongs were short and the end of the putter blunt, the amount of extra damage was minimal and the ball mark would heal in two or three days instead of the month or two that resulted from the usual long tongs and the lifting, twisting, gouging method.

I thought the tool was brilliant. It was kept handy on the end of a putter, and players could repair their marks without having to bend down and get their fingers dirty or expose them to ground fertilizers.

The best part was that it could help keep golf greens healthier, smoother, and better looking.

The board of Royal Precision Inc. was not particularly interested, so in 1998 I secured the rights to the patents and moved on with taking the product to market.

In order to back up my impressions of its benefits with agronomic science, I commissioned several tests at universities including Kansas State and Purdue to determine how much better the GreenFix tool was at shortening the healing cycle. The tests showed a significant decrease in healing days.

During this time I happened to be playing in a Champions Tour event in California. Jim Colbert was also playing. I knew Jim lived in Lawrence, Kansas, and that he had a relationship with the Golf Course Superintendents Association of America (GCSAA), which was headquartered there.

I showed Jim the GreenFix Putter Grip and told him about how it could help golf courses.

"This could really be something!" he said. "I want to get you in touch with Steve Mona and see what he thinks."

Steve was the CEO of the GCSAA at the time. I met him in Lawrence to demonstrate the tool, and he liked it a lot. He also was impressed with the results from the university studies, but he wanted to get feedback from some of his members.

I had already spent a number of years showing golf course superintendents the clear benefits of having players using a ball mark repair tool that wouldn't damage their greens.

But superintendents are an interesting lot. They don't like outsiders, and that includes golfers. I provided copies of the studies to Jim's superintendents, and the reaction from most of them was lukewarm.

Looking to get some exposure in the press, I called Jim Achenbach of *Golfweek* and told him our story. By that time, we had around 100 courses using the GreenFix tool, including several major courses like Medinah Country Club in Chicago. Medinah had banned traditional repair tools and would station a caddie on each par-3 green over the weekends to make sure players had their GreenFix tools and used them correctly.

We had manufactured numerous types of putter grips with the GreenFix tool, so there was a variety of sizes and shapes. The program was a big success, and Medinah president Bill Kamm was a strong supporter.

In researching his story, Jim talked with Mr. Kamm about Medinah's experience with GreenFix. He also visited University Ridge Golf Course in Madison, Wisconsin, and saw how their greens were covered with ball marks.

Within days after Jim's story appeared in *Golfweek*, our phones at GreenFix started ringing. The nonstop calls went on for two solid weeks and showed the high level of interest in this chronic problem.

A few months later I came into our GreenFix office in Scottsdale,

Arizona, and my secretary said a fellow named Bill Ward wanted me to call him immediately. "Did he say what it's about?" I asked.

"He just said to call him ASAP. He said, 'I'm the guy that started SoftSpikes!'"

I called Bill Ward in Dallas, Texas. He said, "Danny, I know who you are. How come I haven't heard about this GreenFix product?"

"Well, we're only about a year old and just really getting going."

He said, "Your product is fantastic! My partner and I think this is another SoftSpikes. We want to help you. We have got to meet. Can you come to Dallas?"

So we got together, and I decided to bring Bill and his partner, Myron Gerber, into GreenFix to see if their experience and contacts could help us grow.

Bill knew Arnold Palmer well, and although Arnold liked the product, he said that he didn't have the time to get involved. We also approached Gary Player, but Gary had had a bad experience with a company recently and wanted to lie low for a while.

Despite such setbacks, we were making inroads and getting attention in the industry, adding courses regularly and opening up stores to carry the product.

Some of the attention was unwanted. A friend called me one day and asked, "Have you seen this week's *Golf World*?" I hadn't.

He told me that there was a full-page ad from some guy in the South who made traditional ball mark repair tools and who was bashing me and the GreenFix product. *Golf World* had taken $10,000 for this guy's ad and printed his false claims.

Bill and his partner worked hard to counteract such incidents. We heard great testimonials from satisfied customers. We exhibited at the

PGA Merchandise Show several years and held seminars and demonstrations at various locations and courses.

The Andy Williams San Diego Open was coming up at Torrey Pines, so I decided to go over and see if I could meet Tiger Woods, show him the repair tools, and offer to donate some of the profits to his foundation which helps kids get started on the right foot. Tiger had the first pro-am time on Wednesday morning at 6:53, so I was there on the tee waiting for him.

Stevie Williams, then Tiger's caddie, came up first and we chatted, sharing some racing stories because he was a racer like me. Then I saw Tiger coming up on the tee. I was about ready to stick out my hand when he said, "Hi, Danny, what's up? How's Royal Grip doing?" I couldn't believe he knew who I was.

I gave Tiger and Steve each a GreenFix tool and walked a few holes with their group and then headed back to the clubhouse.

It was great to be back at Torrey and feel the excitement of the tournament, so I hung around and caught Tiger going for lunch in the players' dining room. He got some food and sat down with a few other players. Tiger motioned for me to join them.

After everyone left, we sat there for at least 10 minutes discussing golf, and I was able to tell Tiger more about the GreenFix mission and how I thought it could benefit his foundation. He didn't say a word, just listened intently, and then said, "Danny, it's good to visit with you, and good luck with GreenFix." He stood and was gone.

The GreenFix tool and the new method to repair ball marks definitely represented a culture shift for many of the players. Old habits sometimes are not easy to change.

That became more and more obvious as we moved through the

early adopter phase and the initial momentum slowed. We came to understand that change wasn't a priority for superintendents, who have lots of responsibilities and issues at their courses. The green committees are made up of a variety of people with different levels of knowledge about the ball mark problem.

One of the big issues we faced was that no matter how you fix a ball mark, the area looks pretty good at first after you tap it down.

However, within a few days the area is a dead brown spot because of the damage done by jabbing, lifting, twisting, and destroying the roots of the plants. Many ball marks never go away because they continue to get refixed over and over again, especially in the areas where the pins are rotated.

Often, I would set up a table by the putting green at a course and offer to put on free GreenFix grips for everyone who wanted to try them. Some 95 percent of the players would take me up on it, and as they came by at the turn, they would rave about how easy they were to use.

Still, here I was, a five-time winner on the PGA Tour and a successful businessman, a guy who had spent hundreds of thousands of dollars testing and perfecting this tool, and I was being treated by some golf professionals and superintendents like I was trying to pull a fast one on them. It was discouraging and disappointing.

Faced with this resistance to change, we introduced a hand repair tool with very short tongs that seemed to be easier for people to accept. It became successful at courses.

Ultimately, I decided to engage a couple distributors of golf products to carry and promote the GreenFix tools. I was approaching 50 years old and was looking forward to getting back to playing competitive golf on the Champions Tour.

CHAPTER TEN

THE SHORT LIFE OF THE TOUR PLAYERS ASSOCIATION

An Uphill Battle and a Tragic End

✦ ✦ ✦ ✦ ✦

Originally established by the Professional Golfers' Association of America in 1929, the Tournament Players Division split off in December 1968 to form its own organization for Tour professionals, as opposed to the club professionals who dominate the membership of today's PGA of America.

The offshoot adopted the name PGA Tour in 1975. The Tour operates a weekly schedule of professional golf events across the country and in many parts of the world.

Thirty years after that first split, players rose up again. In August 1998, as a result of disagreements with the PGA Tour, and after a year of preliminary work, a nonprofit group called the Tour Players Association was founded to "promote and protect the common interests" of its members.

I was drafted as president. Actually, I was running in the other direction, but things were coming to a boiling point between the players and the PGA Tour, and leadership was needed.

The Tour Players Association had numerous disagreements with the Tour. Part of the problem was the all-powerful authority of the Tour commissioner and the nature of the policy board, which did nothing to check him.

The policy board was made up of four independent business directors and four player directors. No player directors actually ran for a position on the board. They were elected based solely on popularity, rather than on business experience.

Each player director occupied a chair at the board meetings, asked a few questions, and did some token work. Their role was honorary; their job was to play the Tour.

Another concern was that when it came to discipline, players were at the mercy of the commissioner. For example, even though players were independent contractors, they had to get a release from the commissioner to play in what was called a "conflicting event" outside the United States – that is, an event scheduled opposite one on the PGA Tour. The commissioner could and often did say, "No way."

If a player persisted in competing in a conflicting event, he could be fined. There was no avenue for discussion or disagreement.

That didn't sit well with some players, and of course favoritism and status played a role. A player with more status might get a release, while one of lesser status would be denied.

In addition to seeking to limit the commissioner's ability to control players' schedules and assess unreasonable fines, players were concerned about financial accountability and reporting. No player ever saw the compensation programs for the Tour's leadership or the documents detailing income and expenses.

They also believed that a pension plan should be put in place. As it was, they had no compensation, no retirement plan, nothing.

Yet another issue was that the documents governing the participation of players didn't adequately protect their interests. Unlike other sports that had a player's association or a union or legal counsel, golfers were out there alone.

Overall, players believed that the board did not respond to their concerns, and that the establishment of the Tour Players Association was the only way to improve things. Larry Rinker, Mark Brooks, and a number of other guys supported the notion that we needed to have our own organization with our own leadership.

But it was a delicate situation, and we didn't want to cause a problem for the Tour or for ourselves. The Tour was an incredibly clean organization, and the TPA didn't want to do anything to tarnish that image.

I wasn't looking to take the lead in the fight. But after a year of being pushed by fellow players, I finally gave in, even though all I wanted was to play golf.

Once I agreed to accept the presidency, I gave the job everything I had. I can't count the number of meetings and phone calls it ended up involving.

Larry was our secretary, and Mark was the treasurer. For legal representation I called Leonard Decof, who had been a friend to both PGA and LPGA Tour players for years. Leonard also had been the legal counsel for PING manufacturer Karsten Solheim in the three-year "square groove" lawsuit against the United States Golf Association.

Being a PING player, I had met Mr. Decof before and liked him. He volunteered to represent us, and he brought on attorneys Mark Nuccio and Dennis Coleman of the Boston law firm Ropes & Gray.

Decof led the effort to file the necessary papers for the creation of the TPA. A mission statement was drawn up and delivered to all Tour members at the opening of the 1998 season, which stated as follows:

> *The Tour Players Association has been established to provide for and to protect the interests of our membership. Our goals include a desire to work together and interact with the Tour staff, tournaments, TV, and sponsors, to implement policies which our association supports and which we believe will make our Tour a better place for all players. We do not intend for the association or its representatives to act as agents for the players or interfere with their individual business interests.*

By uniting ourselves and our common interests, we will be able to have more information...

> *...necessary to make informed decisions about a more equitable distribution of our financial resources. Our association agrees wholeheartedly that the PGA Tour should always be based on performance. However, we also believe strongly that every PGA Tour member who plays in a PGA Tour event has performed and contributed, in at least some way, to the success of the event and the PGA Tour.*
>
> *The fantastic competition, the positive image, the commitment to charity, and the phenomenal shot-making skills of our players have overwhelmingly been responsible for the dramatic success of the PGA Tour and the numerous sources of revenue that have been created. This player's association is based on the belief that all members have earned the right to participate in a fair share of all PGA Tour golf-related income. We believe that*

this association will benefit the players, the sponsors, TV, and the PGA Tour as we move strongly into the future.

The documents explained the TPA's purpose:

> *To promote and protect the common interests of its member touring golf professionals, including, without limiting the generality of the foregoing, interaction and negotiation with the PGA Tour and other entities which promote, conduct, sponsor, or endorse professional golf tournaments, in the U.S. and throughout the world; acquiring for the benefit of its members financial and other information concerning tournaments and the operation of the PGA Tour, and advising its members thereof; negotiating concerning playing conditions, rights, and privileges, and all other matters affecting the rights of its members; and in general doing all things necessary to promote the welfare of its members and carry out the purposes of this association.*

I sat down with all of the top players and they assured me they were behind us, but with a caveat. Their responses sounded like they were reading from a cue card: "We support what you're doing, Danny. It needs to happen. But we can't be involved because of all our endorsements and contracts." That was, of course, a cop-out. They didn't want to become known as rabble-rousers.

Mark Brooks, our treasurer, was both a friend and an outspoken advocate. Mark had impressive credentials, including a 1996 PGA championship. He went on to a runner-up finish in the 2001 U.S. Open and a current career record of 803 PGA Tour starts heading into the 2021 season.

So, you might say that Mark had street cred when it came to

speaking from the players' perspective in the TPA. But other voices were muted. Mark described them as "closeted" members. "They didn't want anyone to know," he said.

I spent a lot of time with Mr. Decof and our attorneys trying to formalize our organization and to get a meeting with the current Tour commissioner, Tim Finchem, and the policy board. No luck.

At the time, no player that we knew of had ever seen the compensation package for the Tour's top executives, even though the Tour was held in a trust by the players themselves. We asked the Tour to provide us with the compensation package of the top 10 officers, information we had every right to see. We were denied at every turn.

Not only that, the TPA was made out to be a group that simply was trying to stir up trouble. An agonizing amount of misinformation was being generated.

"Some of the administration at the time was circulating that it was a union," Mark said. "They would project all kinds of dire situations that would take place."

Things became political very quickly, he added. "It's exactly what we see today. Whoever is in power is going to spin it another way."

During this time, I contacted Larry Kennan, the executive director of the recently formed NFL Coaches Association, to discuss the TPA and to possibly learn from his experience.

The Coaches Association was financially supported by the NFL Players Association, which gave Larry office space in its facility in Washington, D.C.

Larry asked Richard Berthelsen to return my call. Mr. Berthelsen was the in-house counsel for the Coaches Association as well as the former general counsel for the Players Association.

Mr. Berthelsen commended me and the TPA for our efforts to help our players. He asked if there were any Tour documents that he could review, and I sent him copies of what the players had been given.

A few weeks later he called to ask if that was the full extent of the documents that governed players' participation on the Tour.

"Well, that's all we've been given," I said.

"If that's the case, from my perspective the PGA Tour golfers are some of the most exploited professional athletes that I have ever come across."

Berthelsen later elaborated on what had led him to that conclusion:

"Here you have a group of athletes who broke off from the PGA of America decades ago so they could manage their own competition. But now, they are outvoted on their governing board by people who are not professional golfers, and who have never invested anything in the Tour.

The result is that they get a much lower percentage of the revenues than they otherwise would, with the Tour buying golf courses and paying its executives seven-figure salaries instead of allocating most of the money to purses and player benefits. And they are told where they can play and where they can't play and are even required to pay their own expenses in doing so. If the players themselves had majority control as they should, I don't think that would happen."

For a long time, our efforts went nowhere because the Tour leadership wouldn't meet with us. In June 1998 I went to a player meeting at the Canadian Open in Oakville, Ontario. Mark Brooks drove Leonard Decof to the same meeting but was denied admittance, even to observe.

Commissioner Finchem was there. I asked a couple questions, but he ignored me.

Although the Tour leadership didn't see us as a threat, they bad-mouthed everything we tried to do and made life as difficult as they could. To them, anyone who supported the TPA was an outcast.

Mike Sullivan, a player director, once said to me, "Danny, why didn't you show up for the policy board meeting last week in Miami?"

I looked at him, dumbfounded. "I didn't know about it."

"Tim said that he invited you and your group to come down and explain what you guys really wanted."

"Do you think that if Tim really gave that invitation, we wouldn't have been down there?"

"Well, I thought you would have."

"Hell, yes, we would have!"

At one point letters were planted in lockers and signed with players' names who may or may not have actually written them. I asked a few of those players, and they didn't seem to know anything about them.

The letters all carried the same theme: Danny Edwards is doing more to hurt the PGA Tour than anybody in history.

Some players were plenty vocal about us. Tom Weiskopf called us a bunch of complainers and "have-nots."

"Who are these guys?" he wrote in October 1998 on the GolfWeb site. "What have they ever done? They're the guys who don't do anything. It's the power of mediocrity trying to prevail again. They should concentrate all their effort on trying to improve and win tournaments."

Imagine that. Weiskopf believed that the Tour, which I had worked my tail off to find a niche in, was something that I was now trying to tear down.

Berthelsen worked with me to try to educate Tour professionals about what we were offering: an opportunity to gain a voice that they had not had before.

In January 1999 he attended a TPA meeting in Scottsdale, Arizona, in conjunction with that week's Phoenix Open.

NBA stars Oscar Robertson and Bill Russell were playing in the pro-am, and I asked them to be our guests at the meeting. I also invited Leonard Decof.

Berthelsen took notes at the TPA meeting:

> *Robertson told the golfers that working collectively could accomplish a lot, as the National Basketball Players Association had done when it challenged the ABA-NBA merger in a class action antitrust suit they filed in his name in 1972.*
>
> *I told them that they really had but one issue, and that was to democratize the PGA Tour so the players would have at least an equal voice—if not a majority one—on the Tour board.*
>
> *And Decof said the PGA Tour would be quite vulnerable in an antitrust lawsuit since all of its financial records would have to be produced. That, he said, would expose how little players got out of the revenues they generated.*

But this wasn't like football or basketball where players had a union, with leadership and legal counsel, and where players visibly and enthusiastically stepped up to say what could be improved.

Berthelsen's notes continued:

> *The players who attended [he estimated there were no more than 15 were receptive, but Danny still had an uphill battle. Predictably, the Tour portrayed him as an ingrate and a socialist, and at least one of his fellow players—Davis Love III—said*

that Danny didn't appreciate what the PGA Tour and the game of golf had done for him. Another player, Paul Azinger, was quoted as saying that the TPA's plan for minimum prize money at each event was "a socialist idea" that was "antithetical" to the "ultimate form of capitalism" that the PGA Tour represented.

The reality is that Mark Brooks, Larry Rinker, and I were putting our necks on the line to stand up for the players and help bring about some important changes—which ultimately we did.

Meanwhile, the Tour administration continued to do everything they could to make us out to be malcontents. It was a tough time to be playing the Tour at the highest level of professional golf while carrying this yoke around our necks.

In our hearts, we wanted the Tour to be better. And it should have been better, because everybody—not just Arnold Palmer, Jack Nicklaus, and Gary Player—was part of the PGA Tour, even those guys who played mostly to have a good time, those guys who might walk away at the end of the week having spent $1,500 or $2,000 without getting a dime from the Tour. Any reasonable person would know that was wrong.

Unfortunately, the word "union" had long been considered "anti-Tour" in the golf lexicon.

"It was thrown at the TPA so long, so hard," Mark said. "It was said that the TPA could be the virtual end of the Tour.

"But look at the Big Three sports—basketball, baseball, and football. I remember hearing, 'Oh, unions were so evil, they just destroyed the other sports.' That's a joke. Unions have helped boost salaries in those sports over the last 30 years. Players in Major League Baseball make more in a year than Tour players make in a career. That's a fact."

I believe that the TPA might have been what the NFL Players Association or the Major League Baseball Players Association had been 30, 40, or 50 years ago.

And I think it's ironic that the NFLPA became a union in 1968, the same year that the PGA of America and the PGA Tour split.

John Mackey, the legendary tight end for the Baltimore Colts, became the first president of the NFL Players Association after the old American Football League merged with the NFL in 1970. One year later he was the lead plaintiff in an antitrust lawsuit that eventually struck down the reserve system the owners had imposed on NFL players. Many years later Mackey influenced the 88 Plan, which supported ex-players who required living assistance in later years.

> **"Danny was as unselfish and as courageous as a player-leader could be. He quit the Tour, got into the equipment business, and then came back with the sole purpose of making things better for the Tour players, and to bring to light how the economics and governance of the Tour did not give them anywhere near the slice of the revenue pie and the other rights they deserved.**
>
> **"Danny Edwards would have been acknowledged as the John Mackey, or the Curt Flood, or the Oscar Robertson of golf if only he had had a little better luck and a little more support for his efforts."**
>
> ***—RICHARD BERTHELSEN***
> ***FORMER GENERAL COUNSEL***
> ***NFL PLAYERS ASSOCIATION***

Oscar Robertson, the Hall of Fame point guard for the Cincinnati Royals and Milwaukee Bucks, was an integral part of a landmark NBA antitrust suit, which was filed when he was the president of the NBA Players' Association. It led to an extensive reform of the league's strict free agency and draft rules and, subsequently, to higher salaries for all players.

Former St. Louis Cardinals center fielder Curt Flood was pivotal in baseball labor history. He refused to accept a trade following the 1969 season, fought the reserve clause, and sought free agency.

Slowly, these players' actions helped transform their organizations. Though Flood sacrificed his career, and his lawsuit against Major League Baseball's antitrust statute lost in 1972 by a 5-3 vote of the Supreme Court, he effectively led the free agency era and modernization of the game.

As difficult as it was, the TPA did get some momentum. When Tom Lehman joined in October 1998, *Golf World* said that his move gave the group an "instant shot of credibility," and that Tim Finchem could "no longer ignore [the] organization on the basis that it was founded primarily by dissidents and journeymen."

Eventually we were able to put enough pressure on the PGA Tour and on Finchem to get a few of the things we wanted *(see opposite page).*

Mark Brooks remembered some players in the TPA who ascended to the Tour's policy board. A couple of them, he says, didn't fulfill their terms.

"I got minor satisfaction that after being so adamant about how awful the TPA idea was, once they got into a leadership position with the Tour they decided they didn't like what they saw in every case and cut their service short," he said.

Mark emphasized that he was never "anti–PGA Tour."

"If I was, I would have done something else the last 37 years," he said. "All people who worked for the Tour are not evil people. But I honestly felt like the Tour could be better. There had to be accountability for all the dollars."

TOURNAMENT PLAYERS ASSOCIATION ACHIEVEMENTS

(SOURCE: 2022-23 SEASON PGA TOUR PLAYER BENEFITS HANDBOOK)

PGA TOUR INCENTIVE PLAN (BEGAN IN 1998)

Basis of Contribution: Prior to 2007, the top 70 players in each of three segments of an Adjusted Official Money list received allocation of the Tour's contribution. Range of contributions based upon $6 million funding: $4,000–$360,000.

Vesting: Based upon a participant's schedule over a four-year vesting period. Full vesting occurs if a participant plays in 100 events; or plays each event on the calendar at least once; or increases his average.

FEDEXCUP BONUS PLAN (BEGAN IN 1999)

Eligibility: Voting or nonvoting members.

Plan Contributions: PGA Tour funded ($18.5 million in 2012).

Basis of Contribution: The top 150 members will receive an allocation based upon the Final FedExCup Standings. Allocations will range from $1 million for first place to $32,500 for 150th place.

Timing of Contribution: Contributions are funded by April 1 following the season earned.

Investment of Plan's Assets: Participants may allocate among 16 core funds and five target retirement date funds. Additionally, participants with balances in excess of $1 million will have self-directed brokerage account options as described in the Investment Choices section.

Vesting: Balances in the plan are fully vested.

Hardship Distribution: Available for unforeseeable emergency situations as defined in the Plan.

Commencement of Benefits: Benefits begin at the later of age 45 or one season since 15 more events were played on either the PGA Tour or PGA Tour Champions. Benefits begin no later than age 60.

PGA TOUR GROUP DISABILITY INSURANCE

The PGA Tour Group Disability Insurance Program was put into place to provide players with a base level of disability coverage. No medical underwriting is required to participate, and the premium is fully paid by the PGA Tour. Players may choose to supplement this base level of coverage by purchasing individual policies.

✦ ✦ ✦ ✦ ✦

THE DAY THE TPA DIED

THE ANNUAL TPA MEETING in the fall of 1999 was scheduled around the Tour Championship in Houston. As I neared my two-year commitment as president of the TPA, I began to share more of the TPA status and issues with Payne Stewart.

Payne had been a friend and supporter of the TPA from the beginning. He had an infectious personality and players respected him. He believed that the basic issues the TPA stood for were good for the players and for the PGA Tour. He believed the players had every right to see the financial condition of their organization and sources of revenue that all our collective efforts had developed. Payne was interested and wanted to be apprised of the organization's progress along the way.

After numerous conversations with Payne, I asked if he would consider taking over my role as president, and he said he would.

Payne Stewart would have been a big step above me in credibility and performance. Everybody loved Payne, and they would have listened to him more than me. He also would have refused to accept their excuses for not actively participating in our efforts.

On Monday, October 25, I was wrapping up a corporate golf school in Pinehurst, North Carolina. I was planning to meet Payne in Houston on Tuesday morning, two days before the start of the Tour Championship. We had a press conference scheduled in the clubhouse at Champions Golf Club.

As I stood there on the green at Pinehurst, looking forward to our meeting the next day, events were playing out that would shock the world of golf.

That morning, Payne had boarded a chartered Learjet 35 in Orlando, Florida, with Robert Fraley and Van Ardan, two officers of Leader Enterprises, the firm that acted as his agent.

They were joined by two pilots, Michael Kling and Stephanie Bellegarrigue. Golf course architect Bruce Borland also was on board. Borland was with Jack Nicklaus's golf course design company and was eager to work with Payne on building a new home course for his alma mater, Southern Methodist University.

The Learjet took off at 9:19 a.m. Eastern Time.

I was on my cell phone with TPA attorney Dennis Coleman when he interrupted our conversation to speak with someone in his office. "What? Payne Stewart?" I heard him exclaim.

"Do you know anything about this?" he asked me.

"No. What's happening?"

"They say that Payne is on a plane that is out of control. Danny, this is unbelievable!"

Nearly four hours after takeoff, the plane crashed in a marshy pasture outside Mina, South Dakota. It was later determined that the cabin had failed to pressurize, depriving the passengers of oxygen. They probably had lost consciousness and died soon after the plane took off.

At that moment, the TPA ended.

The next day in Houston, Commissioner Finchem showed up uninvited and declared that he would address the TPA meeting. Tom Lehman confronted him, and they got into a heated argument.

Tim ended up going into the meeting, but it was a horrible situation. It was not the time to be discussing our ongoing disagreements, not after one of our brothers had been killed.

The Tour Championship went on in honor of Payne.

I watched the emotional memorial ceremony for Payne and reached out to his family several times. I believe that they would have been proud of what he planned to do that week in Houston.

CHAPTER TWELVE

THE CHIPPING EQUATION AND OPEN ROAD

From the Ground Up to Finding My Groove Again

✦ ✦ ✦ ✦ ✦

From 1988 through 1995, as I was working to make a success of Royal Grip Inc., I played golf maybe once a month.

By 2001, I was approaching 50 years old and was eager to return to competition and the chance to play against others my age on the PGA Tour Champions.

At that time, I was working with distributors to keep the GreenFix Golf business going. There were 20 to 25 PGA Tour Champions events a year, and I was talking to a lot of professionals and superintendents.

It was good to see those guys again. Their greetings in the locker room ran along the lines of "We wondered what had happened to you!" and "Why did you disappear?" I would smile and say that I had wanted time to see where life would lead me, and that I was now happy to be back among my friends.

After taking five years off, I was still competitive. I didn't win any events, but I set my mind to playing and had a good time doing it. I was in my element.

Yet, I was restless.

Early in my career I had learned the art of chipping the ball on the ground around the greens. It became a key part of my game and the philosophy that I applied much later in life to developing a new business, The Chipping Equation.

The story of how I learned to perfect the method begins with a call from sports agent Ed Barner during my junior year at Oklahoma State. Ed's company, Uni-Managers International, managed players including Sam Snead, Billy Casper, Johnny Miller, Lou Graham, and many more.

As I described earlier, I was shocked and flattered when Ed called. He invited me to be his guest in Los Angeles over a weekend to view his operation. I decided to call and ask my dad if he had any advice.

My parents happened to come to Stillwater a couple days later, and as my mom entered my dorm she told me, "Your father was upset after your call. He thought you had already made up your mind to go to Los Angeles and that you weren't really asking for his advice ."

I just couldn't win with my dad.

I turned professional in the fall of 1973, and over the next few years Ed arranged for golfers in his stable to compete in fall tournaments in Japan, with guaranteed expenses and appearance fees. One time Ed asked me to take a young golfer under my wing on an upcoming trip to Japan. "Show him around and keep an eye on him," he said.

"No problem," I said. "Who is he?"

"He's a fellow from Spain named Severiano Ballesteros."

Seve and I ended up playing a number of practice rounds together and events. We were paired numerous times in the ensuing years in domestic and international events.

I was particularly intrigued as I watched Seve make miraculous shots around the greens. He was an outstanding scrambler, and he used horizontal momentum often in his chipping.

One day after play we met on a practice range and we chatted for a bit.

I asked, "Seve, tell me the secret to your chipping."

Seve glanced around as if someone might be listening, then looked at me with those intense eyes of his. "Danny, you have to find the spot," he said, then returned to practice.

I realized he had a method of where to land the ball on its first bounce rolling toward the green.

That was a confirmation of how important and helpful it is to be able to calculate the landing spot for a chip.

There were some players in those days who played the ball with horizontal momentum, but mostly with guesswork and hours of practice. Watching the Spanish legend up close during those years caused me to focus more on chipping horizontally and calculating a specific landing spot.

✦ ✦ ✦ ✦ ✦

IN 2019, I LAUNCHED my latest business venture by formalizing what I call *The Chipping Equation*, a system that I teach through seminars and videos.

My career was significantly aided by learning and perfecting chipping the ball on the ground with horizontal momentum. Unlike vertical momentum, which is highly inconsistent for the vast majority of amateur golfers.

I've noticed fewer and fewer players on Tour, and even college players, using the high-percentage method of chipping—largely, I believe, because of the introduction of the high-lofted wedges.

A few years ago, I started playing professional events on the Sunbelt Senior Tour, based in Myrtle Beach, South Carolina, and run by a good man named Don Barnes. An event was scheduled at the Whiteface Golf & Country Club in Lake Placid, New York, and because I had never been to Lake Placid, I decided to go.

After meeting PGA head professional Peter Martin, who is a legend in those parts, I headed out to play some holes. There were few players on the course, so I started hitting balls off the tees and a few extra chips and putts.

On the third or fourth green I looked back down the fairway and saw someone in a golf cart approaching. I wondered if I had done something wrong.

As he drove up to me, the big fellow with a tanned face smiled and said, "Are you Danny Edwards?"

"Yes, I am."

"I'm Bob Modliszewski, and I want to welcome you to Lake Placid. We're so glad you're here, and if there is anything I can do for you please let me know."

Wow, how nice, I thought. We talked for a while longer, then Bob asked if I would like to have a drink with him in the grill later.

After I finished nine, there was Bob in the grill, motioning me over. It turned out he was a 10-time club champion, including three at Whiteface, as well as a local businessman, a former golf coach, and a really great guy. Bob had followed my career and knew some of my background.

Everyone who came into the grill stopped to say hello to Bob. He introduced me to numerous fellows. We had a lot in common, and I enjoyed visiting with him. We decided to have dinner in the grill and continue our conversation. It was the start of a long friendship.

Because I had come straight to the golf course after arriving in town, I hadn't yet gotten a hotel room. Bob invited me to stay in his guest bedroom.

The next day we played the tight and challenging Whiteface Club. Bob showed me around the course and made some suggestions. He had a good game, but I noticed his chipping around the greens was pretty weak.

The Whiteface course was fun to play, and I met some very nice people. The historic town of Lake Placid has several other courses, including the beautiful Lake Placid Club, which has 36 Championship holes plus a wonderful par-3 course.

The town also is home to the Craig Wood Golf and Country Club, named in honor of the native son and Hall of Fame member who bounced back after being a runner-up in every major in the 1930s by winning the 1941 Masters and U.S. Open.

I was disappointed that the Sunbelt Senior Tour event was held in Lake Placid for only one more year, but I enjoyed the town and my new friends there so much, I kept going back.

Over the next few years, Bob and I started meeting in Naples, Florida, for a few weeks in the winter for golf and storytelling, and then in Lake Placid for several weeks in the summer. In recent years I've spent the entire summer there and have had a blast.

Bob Modliszewski is now 73 years old, has had an agonizing five hip surgeries, and drives the ball 220 to 230 yards.

One day in 2016, Bob was practicing his chipping on the green at the Lake Placid Club, having hobbled there with his cane after his most recent surgery. I walked up and asked him how the practice was going.

"Not good," he said.

I asked if he would be open to some suggestions based on a method I had used successfully for many years on the PGA Tour. He said he would. So, I showed him one of the two formulas I had come to call my Chipping Equation System, with the appropriate club and the proper setup.

After that I went over to the range to hit balls for a while. When I came back to see how Bob was doing, I could tell from the look in his eyes that something good was happening.

`He said, "Danny, this is unbelievable! I've never chipped balls so close to the hole, and it's so easy. I've even holed a couple already!"

One day Bob and I were paired with a couple other fellows, including former Chicago Bears quarterback Bob Avellini, at the TPC Treviso Bay in Naples, Florida, a very challenging course and the site of a PGA Tour Champions event in recent years.

Bob played well and had probably six or seven up-and-downs for an even-par round. I also played well and was 4-for-4 up-and-downs and finished 4-under.

I kid you not, when we walked off the 18th green, all those gentlemen wanted to talk about was our chipping!

Gregg Grost, the CEO of the Golf Coaches Association of America, invited me to present The Chipping Equation to their annual conference in Las Vegas.

After that, one of the coaches came all the way across the country from California to Florida for a lesson. I received a note from her a week later: "In my 25 years as a PGA Professional, this was the best lesson I have ever had. Fantastic."

Today, I love sharing my system through videos and in person at my Chipping Equation clinics at Lake Placid in the summer and in Lake Worth, Florida, in the winter. I guarantee my students that they'll see a dramatic improvement in lowering their scores.

And I continue to try to be a good partner and mentor to those I play and compete with on courses and in tournaments throughout the country and the world. Bob Modliszewski has told me about the feedback he has heard from individuals I have partnered with over the years. "Danny, every person has mentioned that you were the ultimate. They said you took care of them and made them feel special."

I don't seek out such high praise, but I am humbled to know that after all these years of pushing myself, I can brighten the day of a fellow player on a golf course.

For me, a guy who has been driven to meet and work through life's next challenge, I believe there's always an open road.

AFTERWORD

✦ ✦ ✦ ✦ ✦

My life has been a nonstop journey of unbelievable experiences. None of us get to choose the country we're born in, the family we grow up with, or the values our parents try to instill in us. But human nature and common sense teach us certain things: the value of life, the value of freedom, the value of health, of hard work, of friendships, of education, of patience, of thoughtfulness, and of forgiveness.

We choose whether to ignore these values or to take them to heart and practice them.

I was extremely lucky to have grown up in the United States of America and in a caring Christian family.

The older I get, the more I appreciate the lessons my parents, Frank and Donna Edwards, taught me through their words and their actions. These lessons have contributed greatly to whatever success I have achieved.

My hope is that like me, you will pursue excellence in whatever you do. It's never too late to shoot for the best!

If by sharing my story I have brought a smile to your face and given you an enjoyable front-seat view of some amazing experiences, then I am happy.

A NICHE IN THE HALL OF FAME

Danny Edwards was inducted into the Oklahoma Golf Hall of Fame on November 21, 2021, in a ceremony at Oklahoma City Golf and Country Club. The class also included Danny's brother, David Edwards; PGA Tour professional and former U.S. Ryder Cup team member Scott Verplank; PGA Professional Art Proctor; and the late Floyd Farley, who designed outstanding golf courses in Oklahoma and Kansas.

Danny Edwards accepts his award from Tom Jones, chair of the Oklahoma Golf Hall of Fame executive board and president and chief operating officer of Oak Tree National in Edmond, Oklahoma.

DANNY EDWARDS' CAREER ACCOMPLISHMENTS

RICHARD DAN "DANNY" EDWARDS

Born: June 14, 1951
Birthplace: Ketchikan, Alaska
Turned Professional: Fall 1973
—Raised in Edmond, Okla., where his family settled in 1960.
—Exposed to golf for the first time in early 1966, chipping balls on a football field.

AT EDMOND HIGH SCHOOL

(RENAMED EDMOND MEMORIAL HIGH SCHOOL)

1967–69: Member, golf team
1969: Winner, Oklahoma State High School Golf Championship
1969: Selected, Oklahoma Class 3A High School All-State Basketball Team
Owns single-game EHS scoring record (41 points, February 11, 1969)

AT OKLAHOMA STATE UNIVERSITY

1970: Honorable Mention All-American (freshman season)
1971: Third Team All-American (sophomore season)
1972: First Team All-American (junior season) Big Eight Conference Championship
1973: First Team All-American (senior season) Big Eight Conference Championship
1973: Outstanding Senior Athlete (first minor sport recipient)

AMATEUR ACCOMPLISHMENTS

1972: Winner, North and South Amateur Championship Winner, Southeastern Amateur, Columbus, Ga.
1972: First Alternate to the U.S. World Amateur Team (four players)
1972: Qualifier, U.S. Open Championship at Pebble Beach Golf Links (as an amateur)
1971: Qualifier, U.S. Amateur Championship at Congressional CC
1972: Qualifier, U.S. Amateur Championship at Charlotte CC
1973: Qualifier, U.S. Amateur Championship at Inverness Club, Toledo, Ohio
1973: Low Amateur, Open Championship, Troon, Scotland, Tied 39th
1973: Selected, 1973 United States Walker Cup Team (Finished 4-0-0; only player to win all 4 matches)

PROFESSIONAL GOLF

1973: Winner, Eastern Texas Open (with Bill Rogers), Nacogdoches, Texas (First Event as a Professional)
1973: Qualifier, U.S. Open Championship at Oakmont CC
1974: Qualifier, U.S. Open Championship at Winged Foot GC
(Competed in 14 U.S. Open Championships)
Spring 1974: Played Asian Golf Tour
Summer 1974: Played European Tour; Best Finish, 5th, The Open Championship
Fall 1974: Played PGA Tour of Australasia
Fall 1974: Qualified for the 1975 PGA Tour
First PGA Tour Victory:
1977 Greater Greensboro Open
Total PGA Tour Events: 416
Cuts Made: 266 (63.9%)

PGA TOUR CAREER EARNINGS:
$1,212,304

HOLES-IN-ONE: Recorded 26 career holes-in-one:
—18 as a professional
—8 as an amateur

PGA TOUR VICTORIES

April 3, 1977: Greater Greensboro Open
October 19, 1980: Walt Disney World National Team Championship (with David Edwards)
April 5, 1982: Greater Greensboro Open
July 17, 1983: Miller High-Life Quad Cities Open (defeated Morris Hatalsky in playoff)
October 20, 1985: Pensacola Open

PGA TOUR CHAMPIONS

Total Starts: 111
Cuts Made: 108 (97.2%)
Best Finish: T-4, Audi Senior Classic
Total PGA Tour Champions Earnings: $1,471,924

JAPAN GOLF TOUR VICTORY

November 15, 1981: Toshiba Taiheiyo Masters

OTHER VICTORIES

1975: Oklahoma Open
1977: Oklahoma Open
1979: Oklahoma Open
1982: Casa de Campo International

PERFORMANCE IN THE MAJOR CHAMPIONSHIPS

1973-90: Made 25 cuts in 36 Majors (69.4%)
The Masters: T-18, 1984
PGA Championship: T-20, 1983
U.S. Open: T-12, 1982
Open Championship: T-5, 1974

OTHER NOTEWORTHY ACCOMPLISHMENTS

1980: Co-founder (with Roger Penske), Michigan 500 Pro-Celebrity Golf Classic, benefiting Foote Hospital, Jackson, Mich.
1981: Begins Sports Car Club of America (SCCA) road racing in Formula Ford Class
1982: Winner, Greater Greensboro Open in April, Winner, The June Sprints (Formula Ford Class) in a field of 125 cars, Elkhart Lake, Wisconsin
1984, '85: Winner, Midwest Division National Championships in Formula Ford Class
Late 1980s: Teamed with Chris Kaufmann and ran a Ford Mustang in the Professional Escort Endurance Series, earning six runner-up finishes over a two-year period.
1984-2004: Founded Executive Golf Outings (EGO), pioneering in providing corporate executive golf travel. Clients included: Ford Motor Co., Penske Corp., Toyota, Hertz, Worthington Steel Co., Hertz Equipment Co., Mazda Motor Co.
1988: Left the PGA Tour full-time; founded Royal Grip Inc.
1994: Selected by *Inc. Magazine* Entrepreneur of the Year for manufacturing in Arizona
1994: Announced Initial Public Offering of Royal Grip Inc.
1997: Founder, GreenFix Golf Inc.
1998: (August) Appointed president, Tour Players Association; served until October 1999
2001: (Summer) Began competing on the PGA Tour Champions
2019: Founded *The Chipping Equation*
2021: Inducted in the Oklahoma Golf Hall of Fame